AF477153

UNIX/LINUX FAQ
with Tips to Face Interviews

UNIX/LINUX FAQ
with Tips to Face Interviews

Prof. N.B. Venkateswarlu, Ph.D
Director, RITCH Center
&
Head, IT
GVP College of Engineering
Visakhapatnam

BS Publications
A unit of **BSP Books Pvt., Ltd.**

4-4-309/316, Giriraj Lane, Sultan Bazar,
Hyderabad - 500 095
Phone : 040 - 23445605, 23445688

Published by :

BSP BS Publications

A unit of **BSP Books Pvt., Ltd.**

4-4-309/316, Giriraj Lane, Sultan Bazar,
Hyderabad - 500 095
Phone : 040 - 23445605, 23445688
e-mail : info@bspbooks.net

ISBN : 978-93-52300-39-6 (HB)

Dedicated to

*All of Them who encourage Migration to Linux and
Free Open Source Software*

Preface

Unlike other operating systems, UNIX is the one flourishing with many variants or incarnations. In recent years, Linux, a public domain, freely available UNIX variant has attracted the attention of the software/public community. So far, UNIX was believed to be the bread and butter of Computer Science interns/specialists. However, because of this freely available UNIX variant, many people are becoming UNIX/Linux enthusiasts, especially in developing countries like India, China and others.

Hundreds of books are written in the past, exploring various facets of UNIX such as user commands, shell programming, system administration, network management, UNIX internals, device drivers, and kernel development.

In the recent years, many eye catching books became available with name FAQ's (Frequently asked questions) such as C FAQ, C++ FAQ, Java FAQ etc.,. This book is designed in the similar ideals. While writing this book we did use questions & answers from various USENET groups in the Internet such as comp.unix.shell, comp.unix.questions, etc.,.

In this book, we focus on the Linux features and other topics in the open source arena so as to enable the user to face the Job Interviews with enhanced confidence. In addition, this book will be very useful for those who are planning to appear certificate courses such as Red Hat certification. This book assumes that the reader has hands on exposure to an operating system such as Windows (as a user), UNIX/Linux and C programming.

This book contains 4 modules to name (a) Question & Answers, (b) Multiple Choice, (c) Fill in the blanks and d)True or False. The first module explores various mind blowing in depth questions with answers. The questions standard will vary from simple to very standard. Most generally asked questions about Linux also explored. A module on filling the blanks includes almost 500 questions with answers. About 500 multiple choice questions with answers are included to make the students ready for competitive exams and to calibrate their abilities in UNIX/Linux. At the end of the book, about 700 true or false questions are included to test the technical knowledge of the candidates.

Purposefully answers are not given for some of the questions (denoted with Arrows). We expect the enthusiastic reader will answer those questions and improve their skills.

Most of the questions discussed are tested under Linux platforms (such as Red Hat, Fedora Core or Slackware distributions). Unless otherwise mentioned the shell programs are experimented under Bash shell. However, there will be some deviations in our answers because of the difference in implementations of various UNIX flavors.

- Author

Acknowledgements

There are many people to whom I am profoundly indebted while bringing out this book – foremost of them being those thousands of Linux enthusiasts from the FOSS community who actively participate in mailing lists and contribute to the growth of Linux. By its very nature, a book like this would draw heavily from a large number of sources, and it is our pleasure to acknowledge this debt here.

It is also my pleasure and privilege to acknowledge and appreciate the constant encouragement and support that I have received from the Principal, the Secretary, the staff and students of the GVP Engg College, Visakhapatnam, as well as the colleagues, friends and administrators of JNTU. Also, my thanks are due to RIT (Berhampur), GIET(Gunupur), Vishnu Engg College (Bhimavaram). Also, my sincere thanks are due to students of RITCH center, Visakhapatnam for testing the questions in the book.

I would like to express my thanks to Mr. Nikhil Shah and Mr. Raju, Mr. Naresh, of BS Publishers, Hyderabad for bringing out this book with in the committed time frame.

Finally, I owe special thanks to my wife Dr. Sarada and daughter Appu , for bearing with me during the preparation of this manuscript.

-Author

Contents

Frequently Asked Questions with Answers

1. What are the differences between DOS and UNIX?

- UNIX is multi user and multi tasking operating system where as DOS is single user, single task system.
- All the commands in UNIX should be given in lower case while the DOS commands are case insensitive.
- Unlike UNIX, DOS is more virus prone.
- Processor will be in protected mode in UNIX whereas DOS uses unprotected mode.
- DOS uses only 640KB of RAM during boot time unlike UNIX which uses all the available RAM.
- UNIX needs an administrator which is not the case with DOS.
- UNIX employs time sharing operating system. Where as DOS supports a pseudo time sharing known as Terminate and Stay Resident (TSR) programs.
- UNIX supports both character user interface and graphical interface (X Windows) unlike DOS which supports only character user interface.
- User requires legal username and password to use UNIX machines. DOS systems can be used by any one without any username and password.
- UNIX uses single directory tree (/) irrespective of how many drives or partitions are there. Where as in DOS, a separate directory tree exists for each partition.
- UNIX supports NFS to share files.
- Till recently, DOS did not have proper WWW browser.

2. What Makes Linux So Popular?

Here are a few of the reasons - though obviously every Linux user will have his/her own reasons to add.

It's Free

Linux is free. Really and truly free. One can browse to any of the distributors of Linux, find the "download" link and download a complete copy of the entire operating system plus extra software without paying any thing. One can also buy a boxed version. For a nominal price, the CDs are available, manuals get door-delivered, plus there is telephone or online support. In comparison, "home" versions of popular commercial OS would cost thousands of rupees.

With Linux, we also don't have to worry about paying again every time we upgrade the operating system - the upgrades are obviously free too. With commercial OS, upgrades also have to be paid for every time one is announced.

It's Open Source

This means two things: First, that the CDs (or the download site) contain an entire copy of the source code for Linux. Secondly, the user can legally make modifications to improve it.

While this might not mean much to non- programmers, there are thousands of people with programming capability who could improve the code or fix problems quickly. When a problem is found, it is sent off to the coordinating team in charge of the module in question, who will update the software and issue a patch. What all this boils down to is that bugs in Linux get fixed much faster than any other operating system.

It's Modular

Commercial Operating Systems normally get installed as a complete unit. One can not, for example, install them without their Graphical User Interface, or without its printing support -- install everything or nothing.

Linux, on the other hand, is a very modular operating system. One could install or run exactly the bits and pieces of Linux that are needed. In most cases, the choice is on one of the predefined setups from the installation menu, but is not compulsory. In some cases this makes a lot of sense. For example, while setting up a server, one might want to disable the graphical user interface once it is set up correctly, thus freeing up memory and the processor for the more important task at hand.

It also allows the users to upgrade parts of the operating system without affecting the rest. For example, one could get the latest version of Gnome or KDE without changing the kernel.

It's got More Choices

Also due to its modularity, there is more choice of components to use. One example is the user interface. Many users choose KDE, which is very easy to learn for users with Windows experience. Others choose Gnome, which is more powerful but less similar to Windows. There are also several simple alternatives for less-powerful computers, which make less demands on the hardware available.

It's Portable

Linux runs on practically every piece of equipment which qualifies as a computer. It can be run on huge multiprocessor servers or a PDA. Apart from Pentiums of various flavors, there are versions of Linux (called "ports") for Atari, Amiga, Macintosh, PowerMac, PowerPC, NeXT, Alpha, Motorola, MIPS, HP, PowerPC, Sun Sparc, Silicon Graphics, VAX/MicroVax, VME, Psion 5, Sun UltraSparc, etc.

It's got lots of Extras

Along with the Linux CD, normally quite a lot of software gets thrown in, which is not usually included with operating systems. Using only the applications that come with Linux, one could set up a full web, ftp, database and email server for example. There is a firewall built into the kernel of the operating system, one or more office suites, graphics programs, music players, and lots more. Different distributions of

Linux offer different "extra programs". Slackware, for example, is quite simple (though it still provides all the commonly needed programs), while SuSE Linux comes with seven CDs or a DVD-ROM!

It is Stable

All applications can crash, but in many systems, the only recourse is to switch off and reboot (and with some new "soft-switch" PCs, even that doesn't work – we have to pull out the power cable).

In comparison, Linux is rock-solid. Every application runs independent of all others - if one crashes, it crashes alone. Most Linux servers run for months on end, never shutting down or rebooting. Even the GUI is independent of the Linux kernel.

It's got Networking

The networking facilities offered by Linux are positively awe-inspiring. One can use terminal sessions, secure shells, share drives from across the world, run a wide variety of servers and much more. The user can, for example, connect XWindows to another Linux PC across a network. If there is more than one computer, one does not have to physically use the screen, keyboard and mouse connected to each computer - from any computer connect to any other computer, running applications etc., as if they were on the local system.

Salient Features of Linux

Here are some of the benefits and features that Linux provides over single-user operating systems and other versions of UNIX for the PC.

- *Full multitasking and 32-bit support:* Linux, like all other versions of UNIX, is a real multitasking system, allowing multiple users to run many programs on the same system at once. The performance of a 50 MHz 486 system running Linux is comparable to many low- to medium-end workstations, such as those from Sun Microsystems and DEC, running proprietary versions of UNIX. Linux is also a full 32-bit operating system, utilizing the special protected-mode features of the Intel 80386 and 80486 processors.

- *GNU software support:* Linux supports a wide range of free software written by the GNU Project, including utilities such as the GNU C and C++ compiler, gawk, groff, and so on. Many of the essential system utilities used by Linux are GNU software.

- *The X Window System:* The X Window System is the de facto industry standard graphics system for UNIX machines. A free version of The X Window System (known as ``Xfree86") is available for Linux. The X Window System is a very powerful graphics interface, supporting many applications. For example, one can have multiple login sessions in different windows on the screen at once. Other examples of X Windows applications are Seyon, a powerful telecommunications program; Ghostscript, a PostScript language processor; and XTetris, an X Windows version of the popular game.

- ***TCP/IP networking support****:* TCP/IP is the set of protocols which links millions of computers into a worldwide network known as the Internet. With an Ethernet connection, one can have access to the Internet or to a local area network from our Linux system. Or, using SLIP (``Serial Line Internet Protocol"), we can access the Internet over the phone lines with a modem.

- ***Virtual memory and shared libraries****:* Linux can use a portion of the hard drive as virtual memory, expanding the total amount of available RAM. Linux also implements shared libraries, allowing programs which use standard subroutines to find the code for these subroutines in the libraries at runtime. This saves a large amount of space, as each application doesn't store its own copy of these common routines.

3.   Is Linux is UNIX?

Officially an operating system is not allowed to be called a UNIX until it passes the Open Group's certification tests, and supports the necessary API's. Nobody has yet stepped forward to pay the large fees that certification involves, so we're not allowed to call it UNIX. Certification really doesn't mean very much anyway. Very few of the commercial operating systems have passed the Open Group tests.

Unofficially, Linux is very similar to the operating systems which are known as UNIX, and for many purposes they are equivalent. Linux the kernel is an operating system kernel that behaves and performs similarly to the famous UNIX operating system from AT&T Bell Labs. Linux is often called a "UNIX-like" operating system. For more information, see ***http://www.UNIX-systems.org/what_is_UNIX.html.***

4.   Who Wrote Linux?

Linus Torvalds and a loosely knit team of volunteer hackers from across the Internet wrote (and still are writing) Linux from scratch.

5.   What are different Linux Distributions?

Here are some of the more popular distributions of Linux.

•	**Knoppix**	`www.knopper.net`
•	**Red Hat**	`www.redhat.com`
•	**SuSE**	`www.suse.com`
•	**Yoper**	`www.yoper.com`
•	**MEPIS**	`www.mepis.org`
•	**Debian**	`www.debian.org`
•	**Slackware**	`www.slackware.com`
•	**TurboLinux**	`www.turbolinux.com`

6. Can I run Multiple OS' s on a PC?

Dual options like having Windows as well as Linux are possible and one could select which one of them to load every time you switch on. Linux can read Windows' files - it supports the FAT and FAT32 file system's, and sometimes NTFS, so it's quite easy to transfer files from one operating system to the other.

Generally, Windows applications cannot run under Linux, though there is a module called WINE which runs various small Windows programs in Linux. However, Open Office – an open source product loaded on to the Linux system-- can read and write MS-Office files. There are also other office suite options like Star Office, KOffice, GnomeOffice, WordPerfect Office, etc.

Can Windows and Linux machines interact via network? Definitely. We can use SAMBA to share files or connect to shared directories or printers. With SAMBA, the Linux computer could be set to function as a full NT server - complete with authentication, file/printer sharing and so on.

7. Is Linux to replace Windows?

No. It is an alternative and Freely available.

8. Does Shell programs runs under Windows?

Yes.

Bash shell has been ported to versions of Windows implementing the Win32 programming interface. This includes Windows 95 and Windows NT. The port was done by Cygnus Solutions as part of their CYGWIN project. For more information about the project, look at the URLs

http://www.cygwin.com/

http://sourceware.cygnus.com/cygwin

9. When someone refers to 'rn(1)' or 'ctime(3)', what does the number in parentheses mean?

It looks like some sort of function call, however it is not. In UNIX arena, manual pages are organized in a specific way called as sections. These numbers refer to the section of the "UNIX manual" where the appropriate documentation can be found. We can type "man 3 ctime" to look up the manual page for "ctime" in section 3 of the manual.

The traditional manual sections are:

1. User-level commands
2. System calls
3. Library functions
4. Devices and device drivers

5.   File formats
6.   Games
7.   Various miscellaneous stuff - macro packages etc.
8.   System maintenance and operation commands

However, some UNIX versions use non-numeric section names. For instance, Xenix uses "C" for commands and "S" for functions. Some versions of UNIX require "man -s# title" instead of "man # title", where # is the section number. In general each section has an introduction, which we can read with "man # intro" where # is the section number.

For instance, our system may have "time(1)", a manual page about the 'time' command for timing programs, and also "time(3)", a manual page about the 'time' subroutine for determining the current time. We can use "man 1 time" or "man 3 time" to specify which "time" man page we are interested in.

We will often find other sections for local programs or even subsections of the sections above - Ultrix has sections 3m, 3n, 3x and 3yp among others.

10.   What does {some strange UNIX command name} stand for?

UNIX contains many commands out of which some names are little cryptic. However, many have some expansion and of course some are linked with peoples sentiments. Don Libes' book "Life with UNIX" contains lots more of these tidbits.

For Example:

cat = "CATenate"

catenate is an obscure word meaning "to connect in a series", which is what the "cat" command does to one or more files. Not to be confused with C/A/T, the Computer Aided Typesetter!!!.

awk = "Aho Weinberger and Kernighan"

This language was named by its authors, Al Aho, Peter Weinberger and Brian Kernighan.

grep = "Global Regular Expression Print"

grep comes from the ed command to print all lines matching a certain pattern

g/re/p

where "re" is a "regular expression".

fgrep = "Fixed GREP".

fgrep searches for fixed strings only. The "f" does not stand for "fast" - in fact, "fgrep foobar *.c" is usually slower than "egrep foobar *.c".

Fgrep still has its uses though, and may be useful when searching a file for a larger number of strings than egrep can handle.

egrep = "Extended GREP"

egrep uses fancier regular expressions than grep. Many people use egrep all the time, since it has some more sophisticated internal algorithms than grep or fgrep, and is usually the fastest of the three programs.

nroff = "New ROFF"
troff = "Typesetter new ROFF"

These are descendants of "roff", which was a re-implementation of the Multics "runoff" program (a program that we use to "run off" a good copy of a document).

tee = T

From plumbing terminology for a T-shaped pipe splitter.

bss = "Block Started by Symbol"

Dennis Ritchie says:

Actually the acronym (in the sense we took it up; it may have other credible etymologies) is "Block Started by Symbol." It was a pseudo-op in FAP (Fortran Assembly [-er?] Program), an assembler for the IBM 704-709-7090-7094 machines. It defined its label and set aside space for a given number of words. There was another pseudo-op, BES, "Block Ended by Symbol" that did the same except that the label was defined by the last assigned word + 1. (On these machines Fortran arrays were stored backwards in storage and were 1-origin.)

The usage is reasonably appropriate, because just as with standard UNIX loaders, the space assigned didn't have to be punched literally into the object deck but was represented by a count somewhere.

biff = "BIFF"

This command, which turns on asynchronous mail notification, was actually named after a dog at Berkeley!!!.

rc (as in ".cshrc" or "/etc/rc") = "RunCom"

"rc" derives from "runcom", from the MIT CTSS system.

'There was a facility that would execute a bunch of commands stored in a file; it was called "runcom" for "run commands", and the file began to be called "a runcom."

"rc" in UNIX is a fossil from that usage.'

Perl = "Practical Extraction and Report Language"
Perl = "Pathologically Eclectic Rubbish Lister"

The Perl language is Larry Wall's highly popular freely-available completely portable text, process, and file manipulation tool that bridges the gap between shell and C programming (or between doing it on the command line and pulling our hair out).

11. How can I pipe standard output and standard error from one command to another, like csh does with `|&'?

Use

```
command 2>&1 | command2
```

The key is to remember that piping is performed before redirection, so file descriptor 1 points to the pipe when it is duplicated onto file descriptor 2.

12. Why does bash sometimes say `Broken pipe'?

If a sequence of commands appears in a pipeline, and one of the reading commands finishes before the writer has finished, the writer receives a SIGPIPE signal. Many other shells special-case SIGPIPE as an exit status in the pipeline and do not report it.

For example, in:

```
ps -aux | head
```

'head' can finish before 'ps' writes all of its output, and ps will try to write on a pipe without a reader. In that case, bash will print 'Broken pipe' to stderr when ps is killed by a SIGPIPE.

13. How do I write a shell function `x' to replace shell's built-in command `x', but   still invoke the command from within the function?

This is why the `command' and `built-in' builtins exist. The `command' built-in executes the command supplied as its first argument, skipping over any function defined with that name. The `built-in' built-in executes the built-in command given as its first argument directly.

For example, to write a function to replace `cd' that writes the hostname and current directory to an xterm title bar, use something like the following:

```
cd()
{
        builtin cd "$@" && xtitle "$HOST: $PWD"
}
```

This could also be written using `command' instead of `built-in'; the version above is marginally more efficient. While experimenting, one can use echo instead of xtitle.

14. How can I find the value of a shell variable whose name is the value of another shell variable?

Versions of Bash newer than Bash-2.0 support this directly. We can use

```
${!var}
```

For example, the following sequence of commands will echo `z':

```
var1=var2
var2=z
echo ${!var1}
```

For sh compatibility, use the `eval' built-in. The important thing to remember is that `eval' expands the arguments we give it again, so we need to quote the parts of the arguments that we want `eval' to act on.

For example, this expression prints the value of the last positional parameter:

```
eval echo \"\$\{$#\}\"
```

The expansion of the quoted portions of this expression will be deferred until `eval' runs, while the `$#' will be expanded before `eval' is executed. In versions of bash later than bash-2.0,

```
echo ${!#}
```

does the same thing.

This is not the same thing as ksh93 `nameref' variables, though the syntax is similar.

15.   How can we remove a file whose name begins with a "-" of C.W.D ?

The simplest answer is to use

```
rm ./ \-filename
```

This method of avoiding the interpretation of the "-" works with other commands also.

The main reason for this is that all the UNIX commands options are specified with -. Thus when we give "-filename" as argument to rm command it assumes it as an option which is of course un known to it.

Moreover, many commands, particularly those that have been written to use the "getopt(3)" argument parsing routine, accept a "--" argument which means "this is the last option, anything after this is not an option", so our version of rm might handle "rm -- -filename".

Some versions of rm that don't use getopt() treat a single "-" in the same way, so we can also try "rm - -filename".

16.   How can we remove a file with funny characters (other than /) in the filename ?

One of the classic answer is:

```
rm -i some*pattern*that*matches*only*the*file*we*want
```

which asks us whether we want to remove each file matching the indicated pattern; depending on our shell, this may not work if the filename has a character with the 8th bit set (the shell may strip that off); and

```
rm -ri
```

which asks us whether to remove each file in the directory. Answer "y" to the problem file and "n" to everything else. Unfortunately this doesn't work with many versions of rm. Also unfortunately, this will walk through every subdirectory of ".", so we might want to "chmod a-x" those directories temporarily to make them unsearchable.

Always take a deep breath and think about what we are doing and double check what we have typed when we use rm's "-r" flag or a wildcard on the command line; and

```
find . -type f ... -ok rm '{}' \;
```

where "..." is a group of predicates that uniquely identify the file. One possibility is to figure out the inode number of the problem file (use "ls -i .") and then use

```
find . -inum 12345 -ok rm '{}' \;
```
or
```
find . -inum 12345 -ok mv '{}' new-file-name \;
```

"-ok" is a safety check - it will prompt us for confirmation of the command it's about to execute. We can use "-exec" instead to avoid the prompting, if we want to live dangerously, or if we suspect that the filename may contain a funny character sequence that will mess up our screen when printed.

17.   What if the filename has a '/' in it?

Recall that UNIX directories are simply pairs of filenames and inode numbers. A directory essentially contains information like this:

```
filename  inode


file1     12345
file2.c   12349
file3     12347
```

Theoretically, '/' and '\0' are the only two characters that cannot appear in a filename - '/' because it's used to separate directories and files, and '\0' because it terminates a filename.

Unfortunately some implementations of NFS will blithely create filenames with embedded slashes in response to requests from remote machines. For instance, this could happen when someone on a Mac or other non-UNIX machine decides to create a remote NFS file on our UNIX machine with the date in the filename. For example UNIX directory has this in it:

        filename inode

        91/02/07 12357

No amount of messing around with 'find' or 'rm' as described above will delete this file, since those utilities and all other UNIX programs, are forced to interpret the '/' in the normal way.

Any ordinary program will eventually try to do unlink("91/02/07"), which as far as the kernel is concerned means "unlink the file 07 in the subdirectory 02 of directory 91", but that's not what we have - we have a *FILE* named "91/02/07" in the current directory. This is a subtle but crucial distinction.

What can we do in this case? The first thing to try is to return to the Mac that created this crummy entry, and see if we can convince it and our local NFS daemon to rename the file to something without slashes.

If that doesn't work or isn't possible, we need help from our system manager, who will have to try the one of the following. Use "ls -i" to find the inode number of this bogus file, then unmount the file system and use "clri" to clear the inode, and "fsck" the file system with our fingers crossed (Please note that this clri command is not available in all flavors of UNIX). This destroys the information in the file. If we want to keep it, we can try: create a new directory in the same parent directory as the one containing the bad file name; move everything we can (i.e. everything but the file with the bad name) from the old directory to the new one; do "ls -id" on the directory containing the file with the bad name to get its inumber;

        umount the file system;

        "clri" the directory containing the file with the bad name;

        "fsck" the file system.

    Then, to find the file,

        remount the file system;

rename the directory we have created to have the name of the old directory (since the old directory should have been blown away by "fsck")

move the file out of "lost+found" into the directory with a better name.

Alternatively, we can patch the directory the hard way by crawling around in the raw file system. Use "fsdb", if we have it.

18.   How do we get the date into a filename?

The date command can take a formatting string, to modify the way in which the date info is printed. The formatting string has to be enclosed in quotes, to stop the shell trying to interpret it before the date command itself gets it.

Try this:

```
date '+%d%m%y'
```

We should get something like 130994. If we want to   punctuate this, just put the characters we would like to use in the formatting string (NO SLASHES '/'):

```
date '+%d.%m.%y'
```

There are lots of tokens we can use in the formatting string; have a look at the man page for date to find out about them.

Now, getting this into a file name. Let's say that we want to create file called report.130994 (or whatever the date is today):

```
FILENAME=report.`date '+%d%m%y'`
```

Notice that we are using two sets of quotes here: the inner set are to protect the formatting string from premature interpretation; the outer set are to tell the shell to execute the enclosed command, and substitute the result into the expression (command substitution).

Now, we can use either of the following commands to create file

```
touch    $FILENAME
ve   $ FILENAME
```

We can achieve the above in a single step with the following commands.

```
touch     report.`date     '+%d%m%y'`
ve        report.`date     '+%d%m%y'`
```

19. How do we get a recursive directory listing?

One of the following may do what we want:

```
ls -R              (not all versions of "ls" have -R)
find . -print      (should work everywhere)
du -a .            (shows us both the name and size in blocks)
```

20. How do we find files with a pattern, say all c program files ?

```
find  . -name '*.c' -print
```

21. How do we get the current directory into my prompt?

How we can achieve this very much depends which shell we are using.

C Shell (csh)

By adding the following lines to our .cshrc we can customize the prompt the way we want.

```
alias setprompt 'set prompt="${cwd}% "'
setprompt # to set the initial prompt
alias cd 'chdir \!* && setprompt'
```

We can also do the same with pushd and popd in the following manner.

```
alias pushd 'pushd \!* && setprompt'
alias popd  'popd \!* && setprompt'
```

However, remember that some C shells don't keep a $cwd variable; in which case we can as well use `pwd` instead of `cwd`.

If we just want the last component of the current directory   in our prompt we can use

```
alias setprompt 'set prompt="$cwd:t% "'
```

Please do note that some older csh's get the meaning of && and || reversed. To find out whether our shell is one of that type or not try doing:

```
false && echo bug
```

If it prints "bug", we need to switch && and || (or get a better version of csh).

Bourne Shell (sh)

If we have a newer version of the Bourne Shell we can use a shell function to make our own command, "xcd" say:

```
xcd() { cd $* ; PS1="`pwd` $ "; }
```

If we have an older Bourne shell, it's complicated but not impossible. Add this to our profile file:

```
LOGIN_SHELL=$$ export LOGIN_SHELL
CMDFILE=/tmp/cd.$$ export CMDFILE
# 16 is SIGURG, pick a signal that's not likely to be used
PROMPTSIG=16 export PROMPTSIG
trap '. $CMDFILE' $PROMPTSIG
```

and then put this executable script (without the indentation!), let's call it "xcd", somewhere in our PATH

```
: xcd directory - change directory and set prompt
: by signaling the login shell to read a command file
cat >${CMDFILE?"not set"} <<EOF
cd $1
PS1="\`pwd\`$ "
EOF
kill -${PROMPTSIG?"not set"} ${LOGIN_SHELL?"not set"}
```

Now change directories with "xcd /some/dir".

Korn Shell (ksh)

We can this to our .profile file.

PS1='$PWD $ '

If we just want the last component of the directory, use

PS1='${PWD##*/} $ '

Terminal C shell (tcsh)

Tcsh is a popular enhanced version of csh with some extra built-in variables (and many other features):

%~   the current directory, using ~ for $HOME
%/   the full pathname of the current directory
%c or %.   the trailing component of the current directory

so we can do

set prompt='%~ '

BASH ("Bourne Again Shell")

Here, we assign \w in $PS1 environment variable to get the full pathname of the current directory, with ~ expansion for $HOME; \W gives the basename of the current directory. So, in addition to the above sh and ksh solutions, we can use

PS1='\w $ '

or

PS1='\W $ '

22. **How can we read characters from the terminal in a shell script?**

In sh, use read. It is most common to use a loop like

while read line

```
        do
                echo $line
        done
```

In csh, use $< like this:

```
        while ( 1 )
                set line = "$<"
                if ( "$line" == "" ) break
                ...
        end
```

Unfortunately csh has no way of distinguishing between a blank line and an end-of-file.

The above examples takes line of input at a time. However, if we are using sh and want to read a *single* character from the   terminal, we can do the following.

```
        echo -n "Enter a characters one by one "

        stty cbreak      # or  stty raw
           while true
           do
                   readchar=`dd if=/dev/tty bs=1 count=1 2>/dev/null`
                   echo $readchar
           done
           stty -cbreak
```

23.   How do we rename "*.foo" to "*.bar", or change file names to lowercase?

Command "mv *.foo *.bar" will not work because of wildcard expansions: "*.foo" and "*.bar" are expanded before the mv command ever sees the arguments. Depending on our shell, this can fail in a couple of ways. CSH prints "No match." because it can't match "*.bar". SH executes "mv a.foo b.foo c.foo *.bar", which will only succeed if we happen to have a single directory named "*.bar", which is very unlikely.

Depending on our shell, we can do it with a loop to "mv" each   file individually. If our system has "basename", we can use and write a shell program as follows.

C Shell

```
foreach f ( *.foo )
  set base=`basename $f .foo` (make sure that there should be alteast one
  space after $f)
   mv $f $base.bar
end
```

Bourne Shell

```
for f in *.foo; do
  base=`basename $f .foo` (make sure that should be atleast one space
  after $f)
   mv $f $base.bar
done
```

Some shells have their own variable substitution features, so instead of using "basename", we can use simpler loops like the following.

C Shell

```
foreach f ( *.foo )
   mv $f $f:r.bar
end
```

Korn Shell

```
for f in *.foo; do
   mv $f ${f%foo}bar
done
```

If we don't have "basename" or want to do something like renaming foo.* to bar.*, we can use "sed" to strip apart the original file name but the general looping idea is the same. We can also convert file names into "mv" commands with 'sed', and hand over the commands to "sh" for execution. For example:

```
ls -d *.foo | sed -e 's/.*/mv & &/' -e 's/foo$/bar/' | sh
```

24. How can we change file names to lower case or vice versa?.

Shell loops like the above can also be used to translate file names from upper to lower case or vice versa. We can use something like this to rename uppercase files to lowercase:

C Shell

```
foreach f ( * )
  mv $f `echo $f | tr '[A-Z]' '[a-z]'`
end
```

Bourne Shell

```
for f in *; do
  mv $f `echo $f | tr '[A-Z]' '[a-z]'`
done
```

Korn Shell

```
typeset -l l
for f in *; do
  l="$f"
  mv $f $l
done
```

If we want to be really thorough and handle files with `funny' names (embedded blanks or whatever) we need to use

Bourne Shell

```
for f in *; do
 g=`expr "xxx$f" : 'xxx\(.*\)' | tr '[A-Z]' '[a-z]'`
 mv "$f" "$g"
done
```

The `expr' command will always print the filename, even if it equals `-n' or if it contains a System V escape sequence like `\c'.

Some versions of "tr" require the [and], some don't. It happens to be harmless to include them in this particular example; versions of tr that don't want the [] will conveniently think they are supposed to translate '[' to '[' and ']' to ']'.

We can also use perl to achieve the same.

```
#!/usr/bin/perl
#
# rename script examples from lwall:
#       rename 's/\.orig$//' *.orig
#       rename 'y/A-Z/a-z/ unless /^Make/' *
#       rename '$_ .= ".bad"' *.f
#       rename 'print "$_: "; s/foo/bar/ if <stdin> =~ /^y/i' *

$op = shift;
for (@ARGV) {
   $was = $_;
   eval $op;
   die $@ if $@;
   rename($was,$_) unless $was eq $_;
}
```

25. Why do I get [some strange error message] when I "rsh host command" ?

If our remote account uses the C shell, the remote host will fire up a C shell to execute 'command' for us, and that shell will read our remote .cshrc file. Perhaps our .cshrc contains a "stty", "biff" or some other command that isn't appropriate for a non-interactive shell. The unexpected output or error message from these commands can screw up our rsh in odd ways.

Here's an example. Suppose we have

```
stty erase ^H
biff y
```

in our .cshrc file. We'll get some odd messages like this.

% rsh some-machine date
stty: : Can't assign requested address
Where are you?
Tue Oct 1 09:24:45 EST 1991

We might also get similar errors when running certain "at" or "cron" jobs that also read our .cshrc file.

Fortunately, the fix is simple. There are, quite possibly, a whole *bunch* of operations in our ".cshrc" (e.g., "set history = N") that are simply not worth doing except in interactive shells. What we can do is surround them in our ".cshrc" with:

```
if ( $?prompt ) then
operations....
endif
```

and, since in a non-interactive shell "prompt" won't be set, the operations in question will only be done in interactive shells.

We may also wish to move some commands to our .login file; if those commands only need to be done when a login session starts up (checking for new mail, unread news and so on) it's better to have them in the .login file.

26. How can we {set an environment variable, say change directory} inside a program or shell script and have that change affect our current shell?

When a child process is created, it inherits a copy of its parent's variables (and current directory). The child can change these values all it wants but the changes won't affect the parent shell, since the child is changing a copy of its original data.

In order to get our login shell to execute the script (without forking) we have to use the "." command (for the Bourne or Korn shells) or the "source" command (for the C shell). i.e., we type

```
. myscript
```

in the Bourne or Korn shells, or

```
source myscript
```

in the C shell.

27. How do we "undelete" a file?

In principle in UNIX if once file is deleted it can not be recovered. However, systems administrator should be doing regular backups. Check with your sysadmin to see if a recent backup copy of us your file is available.

Refer MIT's Project Athena has produced a comprehensive delete/undelete/expunge/purge package, which can serve as a complete replacement for rm which allows file recovery.

28. How do we redirect stdout and stderr separately in csh?

In csh, we can redirect stdout with ">", or stdout and stderr together with ">&" but there is no direct way to redirect stderr only. The best way we can do is

```
(command >stdout_file ) >&stderr_file
```

which runs "command" in a sub-shell; stdout is redirected inside the sub-shell to stdout_file, and both stdout and stderr from the sub-shell are redirected to stderr_file, but by this point stdout has already been redirected so only stderr actually winds up in stderr_file.

If we want to avoid redirecting stdout at all, we can leave it to it sh.

```
sh -c 'command 2>stderr_file'
```

29. How do we tell inside .cshrc that we are in a login shell?

When people ask this, they usually mean either

How can I tell if it's an interactive shell? or

How can I tell if it's a top-level shell?

We can perhaps determine whether our shell truly is a login shell by fooling around with "ps" and "$$". Login shells generally have names that begin with a '-'.

If we are really interested in the other two questions, here is one way we can organize our .cshrc to find out.

```
if (! $?CSHLEVEL) then
        #
        # This is a "top-level" shell,
        # perhaps a login shell, perhaps a shell started up by
        # 'rsh machine some-command'
        # This is where we should set PATH and anything else we
        # want to apply to every one of our shells.
```

```
                #
                setenv    CSHLEVEL      0
                set home = ~username      # just to be sure
                source ~/.env           # environment stuff we always want
        else
                #
                # This shell is a child of one of our other shells so
                # we don't need to set all the environment variables again.
                #
                set tmp = $CSHLEVEL
                @ tmp++
                setenv    CSHLEVEL      $tmp
        endif
        # Exit from .cshrc if not interactive, e.g. under rsh
        if (! $?prompt) exit

        # Here we could set the prompt or aliases that would be useful
        # for interactive shells only.

        source ~/.aliases
```

30. How do we construct a shell glob-pattern that matches all files except "." and ".." ?

Before we give the answer let us recollect the UNIX wildcards.

* Matches all files that don't begin with a ".";

.* Matches all files that do begin with a ".", but this includes the special entries "." and "..", which often we don't want;

.[!.]*   (Newer shells only; some shells use a "^" instead of the "!"; POSIX shells must accept the "!", but may accept a "^" as well; all portable applications shall not use an unquoted "^" immediately following the "["). Matches all files that begin with a "." and are followed by a non-".."; unfortunately this will miss "..foo";

.??*   Matches files that begin with a "." and which are at least 3 characters long. This neatly avoids "." and "..", but also misses ".a" .

So to match all files except "." and ".." safely we have to use 3 patterns (if we don't have filenames like ".a" we can leave out the first).

```
.[!.]* .??* *
```

Alternatively we can employ an external program or two and use back quote substitution. For example:

```
`ls -a | sed -e '/^\.$/d' -e '/^\.\.$/d'`
```

(or `ls -A` in some UNIX versions)

However, it will mess up on files with new lines, IFS characters   or wildcards in their names.

In ksh, we can use: .!(.|) *

31.   How do we find the last argument in a Bourne shell script?

If we are sure the number of arguments is at most 9, we can use:

```
eval last=\${$#}
```

In POSIX-compatible shells it works for ANY number of arguments. The following works always too:

```
for last
do
x = last
  :
done
echo $last
```

This can be generalized as follows:

```
for i
do
   third_last=$second_last
```

```
        second_last=$last
        last=$i
    done
```

Now suppose we want to REMOVE the last argument from the list, or REVERSE the argument list, or ACCESS the Nth argument directly, whatever N may be. Here is a basis of how to do it, using only built-in shell constructs, without creating sub processes:

```
t0= u0= rest='1 2 3 4 5 6 7 8 9' argv=
for h in " $rest
do
        for t in "$t0" $rest
        do
                for u in $u0 $rest
                do
                        case $# in
                        0)
                                break 3
                        esac
                        eval argv$h$t$u=\$1
                        argv="$argv \"\$argv$h$t$u\""   # (1)
                        shift
                done
                u0=0
        done
        t0=0
done

# now restore the arguments
eval set x "$argv"                              # (2)
shift
```

This example works for the first 999 arguments. Enough? Take a good look at the lines marked (1) and (2) and convince our self that the original arguments are restored indeed, no matter what funny characters they contain!.

However, to find the Nth argument now we can use the following.

```
eval argN=\$argv$N
```

To reverse the arguments the line marked (1) must be changed to:

```
argv="\"\$argv$h$t$u\" $argv"
```

If we allow sub processes as well, possibly executing non built-in commands, the `argvN` variables can be set up more easily.

```
N=1

for i
do
        eval argv$N=\$i
        N=`expr $N + 1`
done
```

To reverse the arguments there is still a simpler method, that even does not create sub processes. This approach can also be taken if we want to delete e.g., the last argument, but in that case we cannot refer directly to the Nth argument any more, because the `argvN` variables are set up in reverse order:

```
argv=

for i
do
        eval argv$#=\$i
        argv="\"\$argv$#\" $argv"
        shift
done

eval set x "$argv"
shift
```

32.   What's wrong with having '.' in our $PATH?

The PATH environment variable value is a list of directories separated by colons. When we type a command name without giving an explicit path (e.g., we type "ls", rather than "/bin/ls") our shell searches each directory in the PATH list in order, looking for an executable file by that name, and the shell will run the first matching program it finds.

One of the directories in the PATH list can be the current directory "." . It is also permissible to use an empty directory name in the PATH list to indicate the current directory. Both of these are equivalent

For csh users

```
setenv PATH :/usr/ucb:/bin:/usr/bin
setenv PATH .:/usr/ucb:/bin:/usr/bin
```

For sh or ksh users

```
PATH=:/usr/ucb:/bin:/usr/bin export PATH
PATH=.:/usr/ucb:/bin:/usr/bin export PATH
```

Having "." somewhere in the PATH is convenient - we can type "a.out" instead of "./a.out" to run programs in the current directory (some of the Red Hat releases will have this problem).

Consider what happens in the case where "." is the first entry in the PATH. Suppose our current directory is a publicly writable one, such as "/tmp". If there just happens to be a program named "/tmp/ls" left there by some other user, and we typed "ls" (intending, of course, to run the normal "/bin/ls" program), our shell will instead run "./ls", the other user's program. Needless to say, the results of running an unknown program like this might surprise us; it may even wipes out our directory!!.

Thus, it is slightly better to have "." at the end of the PATH.

```
setenv PATH /usr/ucb:/bin:/usr/bin:.
```

Now if we are in /tmp and typed "ls", the shell will search /usr/ucb, /bin and /usr/bin for a program named "ls" before it gets around to looking in ".", and there is less risk of inadvertently running some other user's "ls" program. This isn't 100% secure though - if we are a clumsy typist and some day type "sl -l" instead of "ls -l", we run the risk of running "./sl", if there is one.

Some "clever" programmer could anticipate common typing mistakes and leave programs by those names scattered throughout public directories. Beware!!!!.

Many seasoned UNIX users get by just fine without having "." in the PATH at all:

```
setenv PATH /usr/ucb:/bin:/usr/bin
```

If we do this, we need to type "./program" instead of "program" to run programs in the current directory, but the increase in security is probably worth it.

33.   How do we ring the terminal bell during a shell script?

This depends on our UNIX version (or rather on the kind of "echo" program that is available on our machine).

A BSD-like "echo" uses the "-n" option for suppressing the final new line and does not understand the octal \nnn notation. Thus, the command to produce bell is:

```
echo -n '^G'
```

where ^G means a _literal_ BEL-character.

A SysV-like "echo" understands the \nnn notation and uses \c to suppress the final new line, so the answer is:

```
echo '\007\c'
```

34.   Why can't I use "talk" to talk with my friend on machine X?

UNIX has three common "talk" programs, none of which can talk with any of the others. The "old" talk accounts for the first two types. This version (often called otalk) did not take "endian" order into account when talking to other machines. As a consequence, the Vax version of otalk cannot talk with the Sun version of otalk. These versions of talk use port 517.

Around 1987, most vendors (except Sun, who took 6 years longer than any of their competitors) standardized on a new talk (often called ntalk) which knows about network byte order. This talk works between all machines that have it. This version of talk uses port 518.

There are now a few talk programs that speak both ntalk and one version of otalk. The most common of these is called "ytalk".

35.   How can we find the creation time of a file?

We can not find the creation time of any file directly with any command as it isn't stored anywhere. Files have a last-modified time (shown by "ls -l"), a last-accessed time (shown by "ls -lu") and an inode change time (shown by "ls -lc"). The latter is often referred to as the "creation time" - even in some man pages - but that's wrong; it's also set by such operations as mv, ln, chmod, chown and chgrp.

By writing our own program using stat(2) we can achieve this.

36.   How can use "rsh" without having the rsh hang around until the remote command has completed?

For instance, try doing rsh machine 'sleep 60 &' and we will see that the 'rsh' won't exit right away. It will wait 60 seconds until the remote 'sleep' command finishes, even though that command was started in the background on the remote machine. So how do we get the 'rsh' to exit immediately after the 'sleep' is started?

The solution - if we use csh on the remote machine:

```
rsh machine -n 'command >&/dev/null </dev/null &'
```

If we use sh on the remote machine:

```
rsh machine -n 'command >/dev/null 2>&1 </dev/null &'
```

Why? "-n" attaches rsh's stdin to /dev/null so we can run the complete rsh command in the background on the LOCAL machine.

Thus "-n" is equivalent to another specific "< /dev/null". Furthermore, the input/output redirections on the REMOTE machine (inside the single quotes) ensure that rsh thinks the session can be terminated (there's no data flow any more.)

Note: The file that we redirect to/from on the remote machine doesn't have to be /dev/null; any ordinary file will do.

37.　Why doesn't find's "{}" symbol do what we want?

The command "find" has a -exec option that will execute a particular command on all the selected files. Find will replace any "{}" it sees with the name of the file currently under consideration.

So, some day we might try to use "find" to run a command on every file, one directory at a time like the following.

```
find /path -type d -exec command {}/* \;
```

hoping that find will execute, in turn

```
command directory1/*
command directory2/*
...
```

Unfortunately, find only expands the "{}" token when it appears by itself. Find will leave anything else like "{}/*" alone, so instead of doing what we want, it will do

```
command {}/*
command {}/*
...
```

once for each directory. This might be a bug, it might be a feature, but we're stuck with the current behavior.

To surpass this one way would be to write a trivial little shell script, let's say "./doit", that consists of

```
command "$1"/*
```

Then, run the following command.

```
find /path -type d -exec ./doit {} \;
```

Or if we want to avoid the "./doit" shell script, we can use

```
find /path -type d -exec sh -c 'command $0/*' {} \;
```

(This works because within the 'command' of "sh -c 'command' A B C ...", $0 expands to A, $1 to B, and so on.)
or we can use the construct-a-command-with-sed trick

```
find /path -type d -print | sed 's:.*:command &/*:' | sh
```

If all we are trying to do is cut down on the number of times that "command" is executed, we should see if our system has the "xargs" command. Xargs reads arguments one line at a time from the standard input and assembles as many of them as will fit into one command line. Thus, we can use:

```
find /path -print | xargs command
```

which would result in one or more executions of

```
command file1 file2 file3 file4 dir1/file1 dir1/file2
```

Unfortunately this is not a perfectly robust or secure solution. Xargs expects its input lines to be terminated with new lines, so it will be confused by files with odd characters such as new lines in their names.

38. How do we set the permissions on a symbolic link?

Permissions on a symbolic link don't really mean anything. The only permissions that count are the permissions on the file that   the link points to.

39. How can a process detect if it's running in the background or in foreground (interactively)?

In general, we can't tell if we are running in the background or not. The fundamental problem is that different shells and different versions of UNIX have different notions of what is "foreground" and "background". The most common type of system with a better defined notion of what they mean, programs can be moved arbitrarily between foreground and background!

UNIX systems without job control typically put a process into the background by ignoring SIGINT and SIGQUIT and redirecting the standard input to "/dev/null"; this is done by the shell.

Shells that support job control, on UNIX systems that support job control, put a process into the background by giving it a process group ID different from the process group to which the terminal belongs. They move it back into the foreground by setting the terminal's process group ID to that of the process. Shells that do *not* support job control, on UNIX systems that support job control, typically do what shells do on systems that don't support job control.

To know if we are running in the   background, or if we're running interactively we check if standard input is a terminal or not.

```
sh: if [ -t 0 ]; then ... fi
C Shell : if(isatty(0)) { ... }
```

40. How can we tell whether we are running an interactive shell or not?

In the C shell category, look for the variable $prompt.

In the Bourne shell category, we can look for the variable $PS1, however, it is better to check the variable $-. If $- contains an 'i', the shell is interactive. Test like so:

```
case $- in
*i*)   # do things for interactive shell
  ;;
*)     # do things for non-interactive shell
  ;;
esac
```

41. Why doesn't redirecting a loop work as intended? (Bourne shell)

Take the following example:

```
foo=bar
```

```
while read line
do
  # do something with $line
  foo=bletch
done < /etc/passwd


echo "foo is now: $foo"
```

Despite the assignment ``foo=bletch" this will print ``foo is now: bar" in many implementations of the Bourne shell. Why? Because of the following, often undocumented, feature of historic Bourne shells: redirecting a control structure (such as a loop, or an ``if" statement) causes a sub shell to be created, in which the structure is executed; variables set in that sub shell (like the ``foo=bletch" assignment) don't affect the current shell, of course.

However, the POSIX 1003.2 conformant Bourne shells the example will print ``foo is now: bletch".

In historic implementations we can use the following `trick' to get around the redirection problem:

```
foo=bar


  # make file descriptor 9 a duplicate of file descriptor 0 (stdin);
  # then connect stdin to /etc/passwd; the original stdin is now
  # `remembered' in file descriptor 9; see dup(2) and sh(1)

exec 9<&0 < /etc/passwd

  while read line
  do
        # do something with $line
        foo=bletch
done


  # make stdin a duplicate of file descriptor 9, i.e. reconnect
  # it to the original stdin; then close file descriptor 9

exec 0<&9 9<&-

echo "foo is now: $foo"
```

This should always print ``foo is now: bletch''. Consider the next example:

```
foo=bar

echo bletch | read foo

echo "foo is now: $foo"
```

This will print ``foo is now: bar'' in many implementations, ``foo is now: bletch'' in some others. Why? Generally each part   of a pipeline is run in a different sub shell; in some implementations though, the last command in the pipeline is made an exception: if it is a built-in command like ``read'', the current shell will execute it, else another sub shell is created.

POSIX 1003.2 allows both behaviors so portable scripts cannot depend on any of them.

42. How to run 'passwd', 'ftp', 'telnet', 'tip' and other interactive programs from a shell script or in the background?

These programs expect a terminal interface. Shells makes no special provisions to provide one. Hence, such programs cannot be automated in shell scripts.

The 'expect' program provides a programmable terminal interface for automating interaction with such programs. The following expect script is an example of a non-interactive version of passwd(1).

```
# username is passed as 1st arg, password as 2nd

set password [index $argv 2]
spawn passwd [index $argv 1]
expect "*password:"
send "$password\r"
expect "*password:"
send "$password\r"
expect eof
```

expect can partially automate interaction which is especially useful for telnet, rlogin, debuggers or other programs that have no built-in command language. The distribution provides an example script to rerun rogue until a good starting configuration appears. Then, control is given back to the user to enjoy the game.

Fortunately some programs have been written to manage the connection to a pseudo-tty so that we can run these sorts of programs in a script.

To get expect, email "send pub/expect/expect.shar.Z" to library@cme.nist.gov or anonymous ftp same from ftp.cme.nist.gov.

Another solution is provided by the pty 4.0 program, which runs a program under a pseudo-tty session and was posted to comp.sources.UNIX, volume 25. A pty-based solution using named pipes to do the same as the above might look like this:

```
#!/bin/sh
/etc/mknod out.$$ p; exec 2>&1
(exec 4<out.$$; rm -f out.$$
<&4 waitfor 'password:'
echo "$2"
<&4 waitfor 'password:'
echo "$2"
<&4 cat >/dev/null
) | ( pty passwd "$1" >out.$$ )
```

Here, 'waitfor' is a simple C program that searches for its argument in the input, character by character.

A simpler pty solution (which has the drawback of not synchronizing properly with the passwd program) is

```
#!/bin/sh
(sleep 5; echo "$2"; sleep 5; echo "$2") | pty passwd "$1"
```

43. How do we find the process ID of a program with a particular name from inside a shell script or C program?

There is no utility specifically designed to map between program names and process IDs in a shell script. Furthermore, such mappings are often unreliable, since it's possible for more than one process to have the same name, and since it's possible for a process to change its name once it starts running. However, a pipeline like this can often be used to get a list of processes (owned by us) with a particular name:

```
ps ux | awk '/name/ && !/awk/ {print $2}'
```

Here, we can replace "name" with the name of the process for which we are searching.

The general idea is to parse the output of ps, using awk or grep or other utilities, to search for the lines with the specified name on them, and print the PID's for those lines. Note that the "!/awk/" above prevents the awk process for being listed.

However, remember we may have to change the arguments to ps, depending on what kind of UNIX we are using.

In a C program also there is no utility specifically designed to map between program names and process IDs, there are no (portable) C library functions to do it either.

However, some vendors provide functions for reading Kernel memory; for example, Sun provides the "kvm_" functions, and Data General provides the "dg_" functions. It may be possible for any user to use these, or they may only be useable by the super-user (or a user in group "kmem") if read-access to kernel memory on our system is restricted. Furthermore, these functions are often not documented or documented badly, and might change from release to release.

In addition some UNIX people provide a "/proc" filesystem (such as Linux), which appears as a directory with a bunch of filenames in it. Each filename is a number, corresponding to a process ID, and we can open the file and read it to get information about the process. Once again, access to this may be restricted, and the interface to it may change from system to system.

If we can't use vendor-specific library functions, and we don't have /proc, and we still want to do this completely in C, we can use a package named "kstuff" to help with kernel rummaging.

44. How do we check the exit status of a remote command executed via "rsh"?

This doesn't work:

```
rsh some-machine some-crummy-command || echo "Command failed"
```

The exit status of 'rsh' is 0 (success) if the rsh program itself completed successfully, which probably isn't what we wanted.

If we want to check on the exit status of the remote program, we can try using Maarten Litmaath's 'ersh' script, which was posted to alt.sources in October 1994. ersh is a shell script that calls rsh, arranges for the remote machine to echo the status of the command after it completes, and exits with that status.

45. Is it possible to pass shell variable settings into an awk program?

There are two different ways to do this. The first involves simply expanding the variable where it is needed in the program. For example, to get a list of all ttys we're using:

```
who | awk '/^'"$USER"'/ { print $2 }'                    (1)
```

Single quotes are usually used to enclose awk programs because the character '$' is often used in them, and '$' will be interpreted by the shell if enclosed inside double quotes, but not if enclosed inside single quotes. In this case, we *want* the '$' in "$USER" to be interpreted by the shell, so we close the single quotes and then put the "$USER" inside double quotes. Note that there are no spaces in any of that, so the shell will see it all as one argument. Note, further, that the double quotes probably aren't necessary in this particular case; i.e. we could have done like the following manner.

$$\text{who | awk '/^'$USER'/ { print \$2 }'} \qquad (2)$$

However, they should be included nevertheless because they are necessary when the shell variable in question contains special characters or spaces.

The second way to pass variable settings into awk is to use an often undocumented feature of awk which allows variable settings   to be specified as "fake file names" on the command line. For example:

$$\text{who | awk '\$1 == user { print \$2 }' user="\$USER" -} \qquad (3)$$

Variable settings take effect when they are encountered on the command line, so, for example, we can instruct awk on how to behave for different files using this technique. For example:

$$\text{awk '{ program that depends on s }' s=1 file1 s=0 file2} \qquad (4)$$

Note that some versions of awk will cause variable settings encountered before any real filenames to take effect before the BEGIN block is executed, but some won't so neither way should be relied upon.

Note, further, that when we specify a variable setting, awk won't automatically read from stdin if no real files are specified, so we need to add a "-" argument to the end of our command, as we did at (3) above.

A third option is to use a newer version of awk (nawk), which allows direct access to environment variables. Ex.

```
nawk 'END { print "Your path variable is " ENVIRON["PATH"] }'
/dev/null
```

46.   What are zombie processes ?

A **zombie process** doesn't react to signals because it's not really a process at all- it's just what's left over after it died. What's supposed to happen is that its parent process was to issue a "wait()" to collect the information about its exit. If the parent doesn't (programming error or just bad programming), we get a zombie. The zombie will go away if its parent dies- it will be "adopted" by init which will do the wait()- so if we see one hanging about, check its parent; if it is init, it will be gone soon, if not the only recourse is to kill the parent, which we may or may not want to do.

47. How do we get lines from a pipe as they are written instead of only in larger blocks?

The stdio library does buffering differently depending on whether it thinks it's running on a tty. If it thinks it's on a tty, it does buffering on a per-line basis; if not, it uses a larger buffer than one line.

If we have the source code to the client whose buffering we want to disable, we can use setbuf() or setvbuf() to change the buffering. If not, the best we can do is try to convince the program that it's running on a tty by running it under a pty, e.g. by using the "pty" program mentioned in previous questions.

48. Why do some scripts start with #! ... ?

When the UNIX kernel goes to run a program (one of the exec() family of system calls), it takes a peek at the first 16 bits of the file. Those 16 bits are called a `magic number'. First, the magic number prevents the kernel from doing something silly like trying to execute our customer database file. If the kernel does not recognize the magic number then it complains with an ENOEXEC error. It will execute the program only if the magic number is recognizable.

Second, as time went on and different executable file formats were introduced, the magic number not only told the kernel *if* it could execute the file, but also how* to execute the file. For example, if we compile a program on an SCO XENIX/386 system and carry the binary over to a SysV/386 UNIX system, the kernel will recognize the magic number and say `Aha! This is an x.out binary!' and configure itself to run with XENIX compatible system calls.

Note that the kernel can only run binary executable images. So how, we might ask, do scripts get run? After all, we can type `my.script' at a shell prompt and we don't get an ENOEXEC error.

Script execution is done not by the kernel, but by the shell. The code in the shell might look something like:

```
    /* try to run the program */
    execl(program, basename(program), (char *)0);

    /* the exec failed -- maybe it is a shell script? */
    if (errno == ENOEXEC)
    execl ("/bin/sh", "sh", "-c", program, (char *)0);

    /* oh no mr bill!! */
```

```
perror(program);
return -1;
```

(This example is highly simplified. There is a lot more involved, but this illustrates the point we are trying to make.)

If execl() is successful in starting the program then the code   beyond the execl() is never executed. In this example, if we can execl() the `program' then none of the stuff beyond it is run.

Instead the system is off running the binary `program'.

If, however, the first execl() failed then this hypothetical shell looks at why it failed. If the execl() failed because `program' was not recognized as a binary executable, then the shell tries to run it as a shell script.

The Berkeley folks had a neat idea to extend how the kernel starts up programs. They hacked the kernel to recognize the magic number `#!'. (Magic numbers are 16-bits and two 8-bit characters makes 16 bits, right?)  When the `#!' magic number was recognized, the kernel would read in the rest of the line and treat it as a command to run upon the contents of the file. With this hack we could now do things like:

```
#! /bin/sh


#! /bin/csh


#! /bin/awk -F:
```

49. How do we read characters from a terminal without requiring the user to hit RETURN from a C program?

Check out cbreak mode used in earlier examples. If we don't want to tackle setting the terminal parameters our self (using the "ioctl(2)" system call) we can let the stty program do the work - but this is slow and inefficient, and we should change the code to do it right some time:

```c
#include <stdio.h>
main()
{
    int c;

    printf("Hit any character to continue\n");
```

```
            /*
             * ioctl() would be better here; only lazy
             * programmers do it this way:
             */

            system("/bin/stty cbreak");       /* or "stty raw" */
            c = getchar();
            system("/bin/stty -cbreak");
            printf("Thank you for typing %c.\n", c);

            exit(0);
        }
```

Often if we are interested in single-character I/O like this, and also interested in doing some sort of screen display control then the best bet is the curses library which provides various portable routines for both functions.

50.   How can we get setuid shell scripts to work?

Assume we are on a UNIX variant system that knows about so-called `executable shell scripts' which start with a line like:

```
#!/bin/sh
```

The script is called `executable' because just like a real (binary) executable it starts with a so-called `magic number' indicating the type of the executable. In our case this number is `#!' and the OS takes the rest of the first line as the interpreter for the script, possibly followed by 1 initial option like:

```
#!/bin/sed -f
```

Suppose this script is called `foo' and is found in /bin,   then if we type:

```
foo arg1 arg2 arg3
```

the OS will rearrange things as though we had typed:

```
/bin/sed -f /bin/foo arg1 arg2 arg3
```

There is one difference though: if the setuid permission bit for `foo' is set, it will be honored in the first form of the command; if we really type the second form, the OS will honor the permission bits of /bin/sed, which is not setuid, of course.

51.   If my shell script does NOT start with such a `#!' line or my OS does not know about it?

Well, if the shell (or anybody else) tries to execute it, the OS will return an error indication, as the file does not start with a valid magic number. Upon receiving this indication the shell ASSUMES the file to be a shell script and gives it another try:

```
/bin/sh shell_script arguments
```

But we have already seen that a setuid bit on `shell_script' will NOT be honored in this case!

52.   We can not modify the file /etc/passwd. But by running passwd command we are able to store my password in /etc/passwd. What is the secret?

The passwd command will be having its setuid bit set and its owner is root. Thus, when we try to run the same we get root privileges with which we are able to modify /etc/passwd file which is otherwise not possible to get edited directly through command such as vi for which setuid bit is not set.

53.   What are the security risks of setuid shell scripts?

Well, suppose the script is called `/etc/setuid_script', starting with:
```
#!/bin/sh
```

Now let us see what happens if we issue the following commands:

```
$ cd /tmp
$ ln /etc/setuid_script -i
$ PATH=.
$ -i
```

We know the last command will be rearranged to:

```
/bin/sh -i
```

But this command will give us an interactive shell, setuid to the owner of the script! Fortunately this security hole can easily be closed by making the first line:

#!/bin/sh -

The `-' signals the end of the option list: the next argument `-i' will be taken as the name of the file to read commands from, just like it should!

```
$ cd /tmp
$ ln /etc/setuid_script temp
$ nice -20 temp &
$ mv my_script temp
```

The third command will be rearranged to:

```
nice -20 /bin/sh - temp
```

As this command runs so slowly, the fourth command might be able to replace the original `temp' with `my_script' BEFORE `temp' is opened by the shell! There are 4 ways to fix this security hole :

1. let the OS start setuid scripts in a different, secure way - System V R4 and 4.4BSD use the /dev/fd driver to pass the   interpreter a file descriptor for the script
2. let the script be interpreted indirectly, through a front-end that makes sure everything is all right before starting the real interpreter - if we use the `indir' program from comp.sources.UNIX the setuid script will look like this:

```
#!/bin/indir -u
#?/bin/sh /etc/setuid_script
```

3. make a `binary wrapper': a real executable that is setuid and whose only task is to execute the interpreter with the name of the script as an argument
4. make a general `setuid script server' that tries to locate the requested `service' in a database of valid scripts and upon   success will start the right interpreter with the right arguments.

54. How can I find out which user or process has a file open or is using a particular file system (so that I can unmount it?)

Use fuser (system V), fstat (BSD), ofiles (public domain) or pff (public domain). These programs will tell us various things about processes using particular files.

A port of the 4.3 BSD fstat to Dynix, SunOS and Ultrix can be found in archives of comp.sources.UNIX, volume 18.

The pff is part of the kstuff package, and works on quite a few systems.

Also, there is a program called lsof.

55. How do we keep track of people who are fingering us?

Generally, we can't find out the user id of someone who is fingering us from a remote machine. We may be able to find out which machine the remote request is coming from. One possibility, if our system supports it and assuming the finger daemon doesn't object, is to make our .plan file a "named pipe" instead of a plain file. (Use 'mknod' to do this.)

We can then start up a program that will open our .plan file for writing; the open will block until some other process (namely fingerd) opens the .plan for reading. Now we can feed whatever we want through this pipe, which lets us to show different. Plan information every time someone fingers us. One program for doing this is the "planner" package in volume 41 of the comp.sources.misc archives.

Of course, this may not work at all if our system doesn't support named pipes or if your local fingerd insists on having plain .plan files.

Our program can also take the opportunity to look at the output of "netstat" and spot where an incoming finger connection is coming from, but this won't gets us the remote user.

Getting the remote user id would require that the remote site be running an identity service such as RFC 931. There are now three RFC 931 implementations for popular BSD machines, and several applications (such as the wuarchive ftpd) supporting the server.

There are three caveats relating to this answer. The first is that many NFS systems won't recognize the named pipe correctly. This means that trying to read the pipe on another machine will either block until it times out, or see it as a zero-length file, and never print it.

The second problem is that on many systems, fingerd checks that the .plan file contains data (and is readable) before trying to read it. This will cause remote fingers to miss our .plan file entirely.

The third problem is that a system that supports named pipes usually has a fixed number of named pipes available on the system at any given time - check the kernel config file and FIFOCNT option. If the number of pipes on the system exceeds the FIFOCNT value, the system blocks new pipes until somebody frees the resources. The reason for this is that buffers are allocated in a non-paged memory.

56. Is it possible to reconnect a process to a terminal after it has been disconnected, e.g. after starting a program in the background and logging out?

Most variants of UNIX do not support "detaching" and "attaching" processes, as operating systems such as VMS and Multics support. However, there are three freely redistributable packages which can be used to start processes in such a way that they can be later reattached to a terminal.

The first is "screen," which is described in the comp.sources.UNIX archives as "Screen, multiple windows on a CRT" (see the "screen-3.2" package in comp.sources.misc, volume 28.) This package will run on at least BSD, System V r3.2 and SCO UNIX.

The second is "pty," which is described in the comp.sources.UNIX archives as a package to "Run a program under a pty session" (see "pty" in volume 23). pty is designed for use under BSD-like system only.

The third is "dislocate," which is a script that comes with the expect distribution. Unlike the previous two, this should run on all UNIX versions. Details on getting expect can be found in question 3.9 .

None of these packages is retroactive, i.e. we must have started a process under screen or pty in order to be able to detach and reattach it.

57. Is it possible to "spy" on a terminal, displaying the output that's appearing on it on another terminal?

There are a few different ways we can do this, although none of them is perfect:

* kibitz allows two (or more) people to interact with a shell (or any arbitrary program). Uses include:

- watching or aiding another person's terminal session;

- recording a conversation while retaining the ability to

scroll backwards, save the conversation, or even edit it

while in progress;

- teaming up on games, document editing, or other cooperative

tasks where each person has strengths and weakness that

complement one another.

kibitz comes as part of the expect distribution. See question 3.9.

kibitz requires permission from the person to be spy'd upon. To

spy without permission requires less pleasant approaches:

* We can write a program that rummages through Kernel structures and watches the output buffer for the terminal in question, displaying characters as they are output. This, obviously, is not something that should be attempted by anyone who does not have experience working with the UNIX kernel. Furthermore, whatever method we come up with will probably be quite non-portable.

* If we want to do this to a particular hard-wired terminal all the time (e.g. if we want operators to be able to check the console terminal of a machine from other machines), we can actually splice a monitor into the cable for the terminal. For example, plug the monitor output into another machine's serial port, and run a program on that port that stores its input somewhere and then transmits it out *another* port, this one really going to the physical terminal. If we do this, we have

to make sure that any output from the terminal is transmitted back over the wire, although if we splice only into the computer->terminal wires, this isn't much of a problem. This is not something that should be attempted by anyone who is not very familiar with terminal wiring and such.

* The latest version of screen includes a multi-user mode.

* If the system being used has streams (SunOS, SVR4), the advise program that was posted in volume 28 of comp.sources.misc can be used. AND it doesn't require that it be run first (we do have to configure our system in advance to automatically push the advise module on the stream whenever a tty or pty is opened).

58. Can shells be classified into categories?

In general there are two main class of shells. The first class are those shells derived from the Bourne shell which includes sh, ksh, bash, and zsh. The second class are those shells derived from C shell and include csh and tcsh. In addition there is rc which most people consider to be in a "class by itself" although some people might argue that rc belongs in the Bourne shell class.

With the classification above, using care, it is possible to write scripts that will work for all the shells from the Bourne shell category, and write other scripts that will work for all of the shells from the C shell category.

59. How do we "include" one shell script from within another shell script?

All of the shells from the Bourne shell category (including rc) use the "." command. All of the shells from the C shell category use "source".

60. Do all shells have aliases? Is there something else that can be used?

All of the major shells other than sh have aliases, but they don't all work the same way. For example, some don't accept arguments.

Although not strictly equivalent, shell functions (which exist in most shells from the Bourne shell category) have almost the same functionality of aliases. Shell functions can do things that aliases can't do. Shell functions did not exist in Bourne shells derived from Version 7 UNIX, which includes System III and BSD 4.2. BSD 4.3 and System V shells do support shell functions.

Use unalias to remove aliases and unset to remove functions.

61. How are shell variables assigned?

The shells from the C shell category use "set variable=value" for variables local to the shell and "setenv variable value" for environment variables. To get rid of variables in these shells use unset and unsetenv. The shells from the Bourne shell category use "variable=value" and may require an "export VARIABLE_NAME" to place the variable into the environment. To get rid of the variables use unset.

62. What "dot" files do the various shells use?

Although this may not be a complete listing, this provides the majority of information.

csh

Some versions have system-wide .cshrc and .login files. Every version puts them in different places.

Start-up (in this order):

    .cshrc   - always; unless the -f option is used.

    .login   - login shells.

Upon termination :

    logout - login shells.

Others :

    history - saves the history (based on $savehist).

tcsh

Start-up (in this order):

    /etc/csh.cshrc - always.

    /etc/csh.login - login shells.

    .tcshrc   - always.

    .cshrc   - if no .tcshrc was present.

    .login   - login shells

Upon termination :

    .logout   - login shells.

Others:

    .history   - saves the history (based on $savehist).

    .cshdirs   - saves the directory stack.

sh

Start-up (in this order):

    /etc/profile - login shells.

.profile   - login shells.

Upon termination:
  any command (or script) specified using the command:
    trap "command" 0

ksh

Start-up (in this order):
  /etc/profile - login shells.
  .profile   - login shells; unless the -p option is used.
  $ENV   - always, if it is set; unless the -p option is used.
    /etc/suid_profile - when the -p option is used.

Upon termination :
  any command (or script) specified using the command:
    trap "command" 0

bash

Start-up (in this order):
  /etc/profile - login shells.
  .bash_profile - login shells.
  .profile   - login if no .bash_profile is present.
  .bashrc   - interactive non-login shells.
  $ENV   - always, if it is set.

Upon termination :
  .bash_logout - login shells.

Others :
  .inputrc   - Readline initialization.

zsh

Start-up (in this order):
  .zshenv   - always, unless -f is specified.
  .zprofile - login shells.

.zshrc   - interactive shells, unless -f is specified.
.zlogin   - login shells.

Upon termination :
.zlogout - login shells.

rc

Start-up:
.rcrc - login shells

63.   RCS vs SCCS: How do the interfaces compare?

RCS has an easier interface for first time users. There are less commands, it is more intuitive and consistent, and it provides more useful arguments.

Branches have to be specifically created in SCCS. In RCS, they are checked in as any other version.

64.   RCS vs SCCS: What's in a Revision File?

RCS keeps history in files with a ",v" suffix. SCCS keeps history in files with a "s." prefix.

RCS looks for RCS files automatically in the current directory or in a RCS subdirectory, or we can specify an alternate RCS file.

The sccs front end to SCCS always uses the SCCS directory. If we don't use the sccs front end, we must specify the full SCCS filename.

RCS stores its revisions by holding a copy of the latest version and storing backward deltas. SCCS uses a "merged delta" concept.

All RCS activity takes place within a single RCS file. SCCS maintains several files. This can be messy and confusing.

Editing either RCS or SCCS files is a bad idea because mistakes are so easy to make and so fatal to the history of the file. Revision information is easy to edit in both types, whereas one would not want to edit the actual text of a version in RCS. If we edit an SCCS file, we will have to recalculate the checksum using the admin program.

65.   RCS vs SCCS: What are the keywords?

RCS and SCCS use different keywords that are expanded in the text. For SCCS the keyword "%I%" is replaced with the revision number if the file is checked out for reading.

The RCS keywords are easier to remember, but keyword expansion is more easily customized in SCCS.

In SCCS, keywords are expanded on a read-only get. If a version with expanded keywords is copied into a file that will be deleted, the keywords will be lost and the version information in the file will not be updated. On the other hand, RCS retains the keywords when they are expanded so this is avoided.

66. What's an RCS symbolic name?

RCS allows we treat a set of files as a family of files while SCCS is meant primarily for keeping the revision history of files.

RCS accomplishes that with symbolic names: we can mark all the source files associated with an application version with `rcs -n`, and then easily retrieve them later as a cohesive unit. In SCCS we would have to do this by writing a script to write or read all file names and versions to or from a file.

67. RCS vs SCCS: How do they compare for performance?

Since RCS stores the latest version in full, it is much faster in retrieving the latest version. After RCS version 5.6, it is also faster than SCCS in retrieving older versions.

68. What are the Linux desktops?

KDE and Gnome provide a desktop environment that's far more Windows-like than typical Linux window managers and the CLI. Linspire is a distro based almost entirely around the idea of making Linux Windows-like.

69. Can the directory be also called a file?. If not why?. If so what are its contents.

Yes. Names of the files in it along with their I-node numbers.

70. How can you use "cat" to create a file "story" consisting of key board input sandwitched between two files file1 and file2.

```
cat file1 - file2 > story
 enter what ever you want
continue to enter what ever you want
^d
```

71. If we create a link file F1 to an existing file F2 and the file F2 has i-node number assigned as 44112, what will be the i-node number assigned to F1?.

If F1 is a symbolic file its i-node number is other than 44112, whereas if F1 is a hard link file then its i-node number is same as 44112.

72. **If a file F1 exists and is it possible to run the following commands when F2 file is also existing?**

    ln F2 F1

    ln -s F2 F1

    No

73. **If a file F2 is duplicated as F1 through command such as cp; if so, does the i-node number of F1 is same as F2?**

    No

74. **What is output of echo $path in C shell?**

    List of the directories in which **C shell** search for executable file of a command.

75. **What is output of echo $path[3] in C shell?**

    Path of the third directory out of the directories in which C shell searches for the executable file of a command.

76. **Which file in C shell serves as .profile of Bourne shell?**

    .cshrc

77. **What will be the output of the following command? (in C shell).**
    set argv=(-l 12 -b 13 -h 14); echo $1

    -l

78. **What will be the output of the following command in C shell.**
    set v=(-l 12 -b 13 -h 14); echo $1

    null (answer varies from UNIX systems to system).

79. **What will be the output of the following command? (in C Shell)**
    set argv=(-l 12 -b 13 -h 13); shift; echo $1; shift; echo $1

    12, -b

80. **What the following command line statement does? set x="$<"; set y=($x); echo $y[2]**

    Displays second word after reading set of words.

81.   **In C shell the following command displays set p="how are you"; echo $?p**

   1

82.   **What is the equivalent Bourne shell command to C shell command ((program > aa)> & bb).**

   program >aa 2>bb

83.   **In C shell what is the meaning of cat /etc/profile >!.profile ?**

The content of file /etc/profile is written into .profile even if noclobber is set.

84.   **Which are dot commands (in bash) equivalent in C shell? In bash, if we a have an executable (or shell) file, say xyz, it can be executed in current shell by . xyz at $ promt. What is its equivalent in C shell?**

   source filename

85.   **What happens if you set verbose variable?**

Displays each line after the variables and meta-characters are substituted by shell.

86.   **What is the effect of PS1='enter "mail" "vi" or "logout" '**

Prompt will change as enter "mail" "vi" or "logout".

87.   **In UNIX system V how many channels can be opened simultaneously ?**

   20

88.   **What is the Buffer size in Unbuffered I/O ?**

   1 byte.

89.   **What is the meaning of Line buffering?**

Buffer content will be flushed out when new line in pushed in to the buffer or buffer is full.

90.   **What is the file /etc/utmp contains?**

user name, UID, and time when a user logged in, number of logged users.

91.   What are popen, pclose functions ?

To use output of a command into our program. These are C standard library functions.

92.   What is name of the environment variable which stores time zone information?

TZ

93.   Which command gives a one line summary of the command?

whatis

Example :

whatis   ls

94.   What is the output of

for x in .

do

ls \$x

done

Lists all file names of P.W.D.

95.   What is the output of

for x in *

do

ls \$x

done

Lists all file names of P.W.D.

96.   What is the output of

for x in ..

do

ls \$x

done

Lists all file names of parent directory of P.W.D..

97.   What is the output of

IFS=#

  for x in .#..

do

  ls $x

done

Lists file names in P.W.D and its parent directory.

98.   What is the output of

(sleep 5 ; echo Hello) & ; echo How are you.

How are you

Hello

99.   What is the output of

(sleep 5 ; echo Hello) && echo How are you

Hello

How are you

100. What will be the output of the following command line command sequence when executed by super-user root.

(sleep 300 ; echo shutting down ; shutdown) &; echo please logout within 5 minutes.

First we will get a message Please logout within 5 minutes and after 5 minutes we will get shutting down and m/c shutsdown.

101. Does the following commands produce same results?.

echo '**'   (single quote)**

echo `****`   (back quote)

No

102. What is the output of ls .*

listing of P.W.D, parent directory, any other files which starts with dot (.) and listing of directories which starts with dot (.).

103. What will be the output of the following command?
cat x >> x

we will get error message as " input file is output file " and we will loose the content of x.

104. What will be the output of the following command?.
cat x y > y

error message "input file is output file".

105. What will be the output of
if test `ls|wc -l` -le 100
   then
   echo "message one"
   else
   echo "message two"
fi

If number files (entries) in P.W.D are less than 100 you will get message one else message two.

106. "cat hello 2>&1" in this statement what is the meaning of 2>&1?

Request shell to redirect (or append) standard error onto the standard output stream.

107. What is the output of grep '^[^:]*::' /etc/passwd

Lists users who does not have passwords.

108. What happens if you run kill -9 $!   command?.

Last background process will be killed if it is running.

109. What is the output of
awk -F: ' $2 == ""` /etc/passwd|awk -F: '{ print $1 }'

Displays only names of those users who doesn't have passwords.

110. who|awk '{ print $1 }' | sort |awk '{ print NR, $0}'

User names sorted and numbered sequentially.

111. What is the output of the command (C shell) echo a{a, b, c, d }c

aac, abc,acc,adc

112. What will be the output if you echo value of an undefined variable

NULL

113. What happens if you execute !-2 at the command line?

Executes 2'nd most recent command. That is, it first recalls the second most recent command from history buffer and if we press ENTER key it will executes.

114. What happens if you execute !?data at the command prompt?.

Executes most recent command which contains the word **data**.

115. What is the output of ls -l | sed `1p` |awk `{print $4}`

Users group names of all files of C.W.D.

116. Which option is used to search for an expression in backward direction in more command?

No such option is available.

117. What happens if you execute the following command?
man cat | more -100 > catman

First 100 lines of manual page of cat command are stored in a file catman.

118. How to specify to cut command that the field separator is piping symbol?.

-d "|"

119. **If a file (ff) contains 4 lines with characters p, q, r, s in each line respectively, what happens if you execute paste -s ff**

      p   q   r   s

120. **If a file (ff) contains 4 lines with characters p, q, r, s in each line respectively, what happens if you execute command**

cat ff | paste - -

      p q
      r s

121. **What data is transferred by a signal ?**

None.

122. **What is the meaning of p in the first column of the result of command 'ls -l xyz' ?.**

Specified file xyz is a named pipe.

123. **Why number of login attempts within a stipulated time is fixed?**

To take care of hacker.

124. **What is the equivalent UNIX command for DOS command "deltree dirname".**

      rm -r dirname.

125. **How to make a file in UNIX hidden?**

By changing it's filename to start with dot.

126. **What is the output of following command?**

sort - file1

The content of file1 in addition to standard Input whatever you have typed till ^d.

127. If user is not logged in, what message will you get if you try to send message through write?.

username is not logged in

128. Write a shell script which prints out a list of every unique word contained in a file in alphabetical order.

for x in `cat filename`;do;echo $x;done;|sort -u

129. Write a shell script which prints file content in upper case.

1.   tr '[a-z]' 'A-Z' < filename
2.   dd if=$1 of=$2 conv=ucase (requires two arguments) filename
3.   tr ' [:lower:]' [:upper]'< filename

130. What is the output of the following command?
ls -l | sed '2p' |awk '{print $4}'

users group

131. A files i-node structure will not contain name of the file then where will be the name of the file will be stored?

In data blocks of the directory in which the file is located.

132. Both who, rwho gives same output?
No

133. What does the following script does if we assume the program is started with a set of command line arguments?

```
a="$1"
shift
readonly a
for I in  $*
do
cp $a $I
done
```

Makes the first command line argument as readonly. Then duplicates of the same will be created with the names $2 $3... and so on.

134. What is the output of following shell script.

```
set `who am i`
for i in *
do
mv $i  $i.$1
done
```

It adds username as extension to files of P.W.D.

135. What is the output of the following shell script?

**set god is great What ever you say i do not listen finally you are looser
echo $11 $12**

```
listen1 finally2
```

136. Which of the statement will not work.

(a)   a=`P.W.D`

(b)   b=

First one

137. What happens if a blank line exists at the beginning of /etc/passwd file?

Guess ?

138. What happens if a blank line exists at the middle of /etc/passwd file?

Guess ?

139. Write a command to display usernames and number of users who uses a particular shell to name ash.

```
grep "ash$" /etc/passwd |cut -d: -f 1|awk '{print $0}END{print "No.
Users=" NR}'
```

140. What happens it you run the following as super user ?

```
passwd –S   venkat
```
It displays whether password is set for venkat or not.

141. What is the output of the following command?

echo `cat /etc/passwd | cut -d: -f7 | grep bash | wc -l`

No. of users using **bash** shell.

142. What is the output of the following command?

`cat /etc/passwd | cut -d: -f2 | grep `*` | wc -l`

Displays no. of users with their as password *.

143. Write a piping command to display usernames whose passwords are not set.

cat /etc/passwd | cut -d: -f1,1 | awk -F":" '$2 ~ /^$/ {print $1}' | sort

144. What does the following shell script.

for x in `ls`

do

chmod u=rwx $x

done

Changes permissions of files in **P.W.D** as **rwx** for users.

145. What does the following shell script does and in which shell it is expected to run.

foreach i (`ls *.c`)

grep rambo.h $i

end

It displays names of c language files of P.W.D which are using a header file rambo.h. This works in C shell.

146. What does the following shell script does.

for x in *.ps

do

compress $x

mv $x.Z /backup

done

It compresses all postscript files in P.W.D and moves them to /backup directory.

147. What does the following shell script does.

```
for i in  $*
do
cc -C  $i.c
done
```

Creates object files for those c program files whose primary names are given along the command line to the above shell script.

148. What does the following shell script does.

```
for i in *.dvi
do
dvips $i.dvi | lpr
done
```

It converts all dvi files in P.W.D to postscript and redirects to printer.

149. If the following shell script XX executed along the command line with "XX as as as as sa", what will be the output?

```
while test $# -gt 0
do
 echo $#
 shift
done
```

5
4
3
2
1

150. If the following shell script name is XX and is executed along the command line with "XX a1.c a2.c a3.c END" what will be the output?

```
while test "$2" -eq "END"
do
cat $1
shift
done
```

Displays contents of a1.c a2.c a3.c

151. **What does the following shell script does ?**

```
for  x in
do
        echo $x
     shift
done
```

None

152. **Write a shell program to list the filenames which are having world permissions.**

```
ls -al | grep `*rwxrwxrwx`
```

153. **Write a shell program which takes two file names and if their contents are same the last one will be deleted.**

```
if diff $1 $2
then
rm $2
fi
```

154. **Explain what happens if you run the following shell script.**

```
I=1
for i in $*
do
J=1
for j in $*
if [  $I -ne $J  ]
then
if diff $i $j
        then
  rm $j
else
J=`expr $J + 1`
fi
fi
done
I=`expr $I + 1`
```

done
echo $I

It removes all files except the last one. We will get some error messages such as file not there etc.,.

155. Write a shell program such that files (only) of P.W.D will contain PID of the current shell (in which shell script is running) as their extension.

```
for x in `ls`
do
if [ ! -d $x ]
  then
     mv $x $x.$$
fi
done
```

156. Write a shell script whenever a file is created using vi its name should contain PID of the shell at that time.

Create a shell file with name vi and keep the same in /bin directory such that it will be activated before actual vi in /usr/bin gets started. (probably you need root privileges to do this).

The shell file (vi) should contain the following line

```
/usr/bin/vi $1.$$
```

157. Two files (file 1, file 2) contains a list of words to be searched and list of filenames respectively. Write a shell script which display search word and its no. of occurrences over all the files as a tabular fashion.

```
echo "Word Filename Ocurrences"
for x in `cat file1`
  do
     for y in `cat file2`
       do
          I=0
          for z in `cat $y`
             do
```

```
                              if [  "$x" == "$z" ]
                                then
                                       I=`expr $I + 1`
                                fi
                          done
                  echo $x   $y $I
          done
      done
```

158. **Two files (file1, file2) contains a list of words to be searched and list of filenames respectively. Write a shell script which display search word and number of its occurrences over all the files   as a table.**

```
          echo "Word  Occurrences"
          for  x  in `cat file1`
            do
              I=0
               for y in `cat file2`
                 do
                   for z in `cat $y`
                      do
                           if [  "$x" == "$z" ]
                             then
                                    I=`expr $I + 1`
                      fi
                      done

                   done
                echo $x   $I
          done
```

159. **Write a shell script which moves files with extension c to prg_directory, executable files to bin directory and files with extension h to include directory and others are removed.**

In C shell

```
          mkdir bin
```

```
mkdir include
mkdir prg
mv *.c prg
mv *.h include
for x in *
if [ -x  $x ]
then
mv $x bin
fi
done
rm *.*
rm *
```

160. Write a shell script which removes all dvi, post script from users home directories.

C Shell :

```
cd /home
foreach i
rm $i/*.dvi
rm $i/*.ps
done
```

(assuming all users directories are in /home)

Alternatively, in Bourne Shell we can use the following.

```
for x in `cut -f6 /etc/passwd`
do
if [ -d $x ]
then
  rm $x/*.dvi
  rm $x/*.ps
fi
done
```

(assuming 6th field of /etc/password file is the users home directory)

161. **Write a shell script which accepts in command line user's name and informs you as soon as he/she log into system.**

```
uname=$1
while :
do
who | grep "$uname">/dev/null
if [ $? –eq 0 ]
  then
    echo $uname is logged in
    exit
    else
    sleep 60
 fi
done
```

162. **Write a shell script which takes email addresses from a file abc and informs whether any emails are received from the email addresses mentioned in the file.**

```
for x in ` cat abc`
  do
  if grep "^From" $MAIL|grep $x > /dev/null
  then
    echo $x mail available
  fi
  done
```

163. **Write a shell script which lists the filenames of a directory (reading permissions are assumed to be available) which contains more than specified no of characters.**

```
read size
foreach x
do
y=`wc -c $x`
if [ $y -gt $size ]
echo $x
fi
done
```

164. Write a shell script which displays names of c programs which uses a specified function.

```
read functname
for prog in *.c
do
if grep $functname $prog
  then
     echo $prog
fi
done
```

165. What is the output of the following shell program?

```
a=*
echo $a
echo "$a"
echo `$a`
```

All files of C.W.D is displayed. Then '*' will be displayed. Then $a will be displayed.

166. What is the output of

```
a=.
echo $a
echo "$a"
```

Simply, . will be displayed with both the echo commands.

167. What is the output of the following shell script?

```
x=1
for I in .
 do
     x=`expr $x + 1`
done
echo $x
```

Two(2)

168. Write a shell script to prepare users particulars by appending .plan file of each user by traversing to each ones directory (assume only users directories are in /home directory).

```
cd /home
echo details of users > details
for x in *
cat $x/.plan >> details
done
echo done
```

169. Write a shell script which says Good Morning, Good Evening, Good Afternoon depending on the present time.

```
x=`date|awk '{ print $4 }' |awk -F: '{ print $1 }'`

if [ $x -lt 3 ]
 then
  echo "Good Night"
elif [ $x -lt 12 ]
 then
  echo "Good Morning"
elif [ $x -lt 16 ]
 then
  echo "Good Evening"
elif [ $x -lt 22 ]
 then
  echo "Good Night"
fi
```

170. Write a shell script which displays names of the directories in PATH one line each.

```
IFS=:
set `echo $PATH`
for i in $*
do
```

```
            echo $i
        done
```

Alternatively

```
        IFS=:
        for i in $PATH
          do
          echo $i
        done
```

171. Write a shell script which displays UID of the recently created user.

```
        IFS=:
        set `tail -1 /etc/passwd`
        echo $3
```

172. What is the output of the following shell script.

```
        for  x in .#..
            do
                echo $x
            done
```

Displays

.

..

173. Write a shell script to check weather any directory is used more than once in PATH environment variable or not.

```
        IFS=:
        set `echo $PATH`
        I=0
        for x in $*
```

```
do
J=0
for y in $*
if [ $J –ne $I ]
then
if [ "$x" == "$y" ]
then
echo yes
exit
fi
fi
J=`expr $J+1`
done
I=`expr $I+1`
done
echo NO
```

174. Write a shell script to find weather a specified user is a legal user of the machine or not.

```
read uname
if grep `^$uname` /etc/passwd
then
echo yes
else
echo no
fi
```

175. What is the output of the following script

```
I=1
for x in `cat filename`
do
I=`expr $I+1`
done
echo $I
```

Number of words in the file "filename".

176. Write a shell script to know now many users are running a particular command.

```
read cmdname
echo `ps -al | grep $cmdname | wc -l`
```

177. What is the output of the following shell script.

```
IFS=#
for  x in .#..
  do
      echo $x
  done
```

Displays

∴

178. What will be the output of the following shell program block if execute with **Ravi Rani Raju Reno** as command line arguments.

```
for x
do
echo $x
done
for x in "$*"
do
echo $x
done
for x in *
do
echo $x
done
```

Ravi
Rani
Raju
Reno
Ravi Rani Raju Reno
All files of current directory

179. Write a shell program which display username of the user who is logged in earlier than any one.

```
echo `who | sort -n +4 | head -1`
```

180. What happens if you execute the following script.

```
Enter Database file name
read namefile

echo Please enter each person name
echo When finished type CTRL D

while read person
   do
     echo $person >>$namefile
   done
   echo $namefile contains names
   cat $namefile
```

It takes a set of names till you enter CTRL+D and lists all of them when CTRL+D is pressed.

181. A file (ABC) having a list of search words. Write a program that takes a file name as command line argument and print's success if at least one line of the file contains all the search words of ABC otherwise display failure.

```
cat $1 | while read xx
do
FLAG=1
for y in `cat ABC`
do
if ! grep $y $xx
then
FLAG=0
break
```

```
                        fi
                        done
                        if $FLAG -eq 1
                        then
                        echo "SUCCESS"
                        exit
                        fi
                        done
                        echo "FAILURE"
```

182. What will be the output of the following shell script?

```
for x
do
if [ ! -s $x -a -f $x ]
then
echo $x
fi
done>list
```

File list will be created which contains names of the files whose size is more than zero bytes.

183. Write a shell program when your program "fem" starts executing, terminal should be locked such that Del, Crtl-d keys should not work till your program is successfully completed.

```
trap "  " 1 2 3
echo Important FEM program is being executed.
echo don't Disturb
if fem then
stty sane
fi
```

184. Write a shell script to lock your terminal till you enter a password say "xxxxxx".

```
trap "  " 1 2 3
echo terminal locked
```

```
while :
do
echo Enter password
stty -echo
read pw
 if [ $pw == "xxxxxx" ]
  then
   exit
  fi
stty sane
done
```

185. Write a shell script which accepts 10 times a password. If the user enters correctly then displays Success else it simply exits.

```
I=0
while [ $I –le 10 ]
do
read pw
if [ $pw == "xxxxxx" ]
then
      echo Success
   exit
  fi
I = 'expr $I  + 1'
done
```

186. The following lines in file abc and is having world permissions and its name is entered in /etc/profile file. What happens?

```
case $LOGNAME in
guest) echo "It is common directory. don't disturb files" ; ;
 root) echo "Don't be Biased"; ;
   *) echo "Don't waste your time on internet" ; ;
esac
```

If the username is guest first message will display at the login time, whereas if root logs in then the second message is displayed otherwise the third one is displayed.

187. Write a shell script which removes empty files from PWD and changes other files time stamps to current time in the PWD.

```
for x in .
do
if [ -f $x ]
then
   if [ -s  $x ]
     then
         touch $x
     else
         rm $x
   fi
fi
done
```

188. What is the output of the following shell script.

```
tdir=/tmp
echo using ${tdir-/user/tmp}
echo $tdir
```

/tmp

189. What is the output of the following shell script.

```
p=10
q=p
echo`$!p`
```

Error

190. What is the output of

```
x=22
y=x
```

```
echo $!x
```

```
echo $X=22
22=22
```

191. What is the output of the shell program (abc) whose content is as follows.

```
usage="usage: $0 [options]...
- -help display help
- -version display version"
echo "$usage"
usage: abc [options]...
-- help display help
--version display version
```

192. What is the output of the following program ?

```
for m in 1 2 3 4 5
do
  echo $m
done
```

It will prints 1, 2, 3, 4, 5 in one line each

193. What happen if you run the following shell script?

```
while [ $# -ne 0 ]
do
  if [ -f $1 ]
  then
      echo " is a file"
  else
      echo "not a file"
  fi
  shift
done
```

Takes a set of names along the command line and displays whether they are files or not.

194. **Explain what the following shell script does.**

```
#!/bin/sh
for i in *
do
case "`sed 1q $i`" in
"#!/bin/sh")echo "shell script"
; ;
*) echo "Not shell program"
esac
done
```

Files in PWD will scanned and if they are shell programs, they will be displayed so.

195. **When a new file created it should have rw– permissions for user and others no permissions, to group, then what will be the new mask value**

161

196. **To find file names in the entire system whose set-user-id's is set, which command we can use?**

find /| -type f -a -perm -4000 -print

197. **What will be the output of the following command.**
find / \(-type b -o type c \) -print

Prints the device file names in the file system.

198. **What will be the output of the command**
find / -perm -2 -print

Displays all files which are world writable in the file system.

199. **What will be the output of the command.**
find / -nogroup -print

Lists files which are not belongs to non-existing groups

200. **How to delete files using find command whose names are .rhosts and are in /home directory.**

```
find /home –name . rhosts -exec rm -f {} \;
```

201. **A UNIX i-node has 10 direct addresses,   as well as addresses of single, double, and triple indirect blocks. If each of the blocks hold 256 addresses, what is the size of the largest file that can be handled assuming that a disk block is 1K?**

$$((256 \times 256 \times 256 + 256 \times 256 + 256) + 10) \text{ KB}$$

202. **With 1 KB block size and usual i-node structure what is the maximum file size we can have in UNIX.**

(17GB)

203. **Which is executed first .profile of your home directory or /etc/profile ?**

```
/etc/profile
```

204. **Write a shell script which displays path of a command's executable file. This shell program takes an executable filename along command line.**

```
echo $PATH | awk -F: `{for(i=1; i<=NF;  i++) print $i}`>/tmp/pla
for x in ` cat /tmp/pla`
do
if[ -d $x ]
then
cd $x
if  ls $1
then
echo $x
  exit
        fi
fi
done
```

205. **Write a awk script to display users name who is working from a specified hour(irrespective of date).**

```
who |awk '{print $1 $5}' - |awk -F ":" '{print $1}' - > /tmp/aaa
echo Enter hour after which users logged in
read hr
 awk '{ if ($2 >= $hr) print $1 }' /tmp/aaa
```

206. **Explain what happen if you run this shell script?.**

```
#!/bin/sh
usage="usage:
        --help   display help
        --opt    display options"
case $# in
    1)
        case "$1" in
          --help) echo "$usage"; exit 0; ;
          --opt) echo "1 for kill"; ;
                exit 0;;
  *) echo "$usage"; exit 0;-;
    esac
```

If the above shell program name is assumed as **XX,** if you enter XX at command line without arguments or with option **--help it** will display the following message.

```
--help   display help
--opt    display options
```

otherwise it will display the following message.

1 for kill

207. **/etc/passwd file is read only for users other than super users. Then how come a user can change his password by running passwd command which alters /etc/passwd file ?**

/bin/passwd executable command "set-uid" is set to root. Thus any user who runs this command will get permissions same as root and thus he can modify ——/etc/passwd file.

208. When you executed vi & command you will get a message stopped TTY output vi. What is the meaning?

vi is interactive program which can only run in foreground.

209. If the file system block size is 8KB, and disk block size is 512 bytes. What is the minimum file size for which data is stored continuously in physical media.

8 KB

210. Write a shell script which lists users names who use a specified shell.

cat /etc/passwd | awk -F":" '{ print $1 $7 }' > /tmp/aa
echo Enter shell name to be checked
read shl
awk ' $1 ~ $shl {print $1}' /tmp/aa

211. Which system calls are necessary for shell to execute any external command?

fork, exec( )

212. What is the use of rcs (revision control system) program ?.

rcs are used to save files at various times such that we can retrieve the content of files at any specified time.

213. What is the relation ship between maximum no of i-nodes and maximum number of files/directories which we can create in a file system?

Maximum number of **i-node**s defines maximum no of files/directories we can create in a file system.

214. If you have a shell script (abc) which changes some environment variable and if it is needed to run to change environment variable of current shell what we have to do.

. abc

215. Write a shell script which behaves similar to DOS deltree command,

```
if [ $# -ne $1 ]
then
        echo directory name is required
        exit (-1)
elif [ ! -d $1 ]
then
    echo directory not found
    exit (-2);
else
  rm -r $1
  fi
```

216. A university computer center maintains with the following format name|address|dept|status|class|telephone no|source of funds|username in the file /usr/lib/database. Write program which takes search name, dept and displays name, address, telephone number.

```
echo Enter search name
read sname
echo Enter department
read dept
awk -F| ‘ $1 ~ /’$sname’/ && $3 ~ /’$dept’/ {print $1, $2, $6}’
/usr/lib/database
```

217. What will the output of umask 777; mkdir aaa; ls -l aaa?

```
permission denied.
```

218. What happens is you execute following commands in sequence?

```
X=$PATH
PATH=
ls
x=
PATH=$PATH
ls
```

Initially a shell variable x is defined and its value is set as PATH environment variable and PATH environment variable is made null. Thus When ls command is executed command not found or bad command will get displayed. Later PATH is again set to original value by PATH=$X. Thus, last ls command will work.

219. What will be the effect of the following command.

sed "s/;//g" a.c. b.c

all ; in the file a.c will be removed and file is copied to b.c

220. If you try to compile a file without main body What error message you will get?

ld: undefined --main.

221. Write shell script using date that prints the usual 'date' output as default but which has options for printing just time, just day-month-year or just day of the week.

```
case $# in
o) date ;;
*)
        case $1 in
        –[dD]) date '+%d';;
        –[mM]) date '+%m';;
        –[yY]) date '+%y';;
        esac
        ;;
esac
```

222. What is the difference between high level language if construct and if construct of shell script ?

In shell, the if construct is versatile as it is possible to compare strings, values and also checks the exit status of commands.

223. How will you copy and paste specified number of lines from one file to another in vi editor?

With the help of named buffers.

224. Write a awk script which accepts the output of ls -l command and lists all the files in the current directory and also displays the total bytes and total number of files in the directory. The script should only print the names of the directories if found any. The output should be in the following format:

```
BYTES      FILE
882        ch01
1171       ch03
1987       com.txt
6041       combine.idx
<dir>      tmp
1178       test.c
Total : 12459 bytes  (5 files)
```

225. If a awk script is in a file, how to pass command line parameters to the awk script.?

Enclosed in single quotes. $1, $2 signifies awk field where as '$1', '$2' signifies command line arguments.

226. Consider a line in which each line has the following format:

<first name><one space><middle initial><one space><surname><more than one space><telephone no>. Write the command to sort the file in the order of surnames; first names and middle initials.

```
sort +2 -3 +1 -3  filename
```

227. Discuss the trap command in detail giving example of its effective usage.

```
trap command is used to trap some signals such as CTRL+C, CTRl+D.
Sample command to do is:
    trap `some command` 1 2
```

228. What does the following script does if we give a set of names along command line?

```
while test $# -ne 0
```

```
        do
          xyz=`find / -name $1 -print 2>/dev/null`
          y=1
          for i in $xyz
          do
            mybasename=`basename $i`
            cp $i $HOME/copies/$mybasename.$y
            y=`expr $y + 1`
          done
          shift
        done
```

This program takes a set of names along the command line. It takes these names one after another and with the help of find command if finds the directories in the whole file system where files are available with that name. All of them are copied to $HOME/copies directory with their basename and extension as 1 or 2 or 3 etc.,

229. who >/tmp/who_out

```
        sort +4n /tmp/who_out
```

Write command(s) to perform the above without creating any file.

```
        who|sort +4n|tee /tmp/who_out
```

230. How will you run commands p1 and p2 such that p2 is executed only if p1 is unsuccessful.

```
        p1||p2
```

231. What information is saved in SUPER BLOCK of a file system (S5 file system)?

I-node, free data blocks information.

232. Using "find" and "tar" utilities write the command to backup all files that were modified last week on the device /dev/fd096.

```
tar    –cvf  ww.tar      `find /      –ctime    7      –print
```
Here, ww.tar is the tar archive file.

233. How will you check the command you have just executed was successful or not?

If the output of echo $? is zero then the command is successful otherwise it is failed.

234. What is the difference between open() and fopen()?

Open is a system call whereas fopen is a C library function.

235. How shall you change a foreground job/process into a background job/process in C-Shell?

Using fg and bg commands.

236. Differentiate between a Boot Block and Super Block.

In boot block we will have bootstrap program if the partition is bootable and whereas in super-block disk related information such as disk geometry and free blocks list is available.

237. How can you access command line arguments and environment variables in your C-Programs?

```
main( int n, char **a, char **b )
    {


    }
```

a[0], a[1],... becomes pointers to command line arguments whereas
b[0], b[1].... becomes pointers to environment variables.

238. What is the difference between file descriptors and file pointers?

File pointers are related to standard library functions and where as descriptors are related to system calls. Program written using file pointers are portable.

239. Explain what happens when a user executes a 'set-uid' program owned by another user.

User gets privileges of the owner of the program.

240. Do you get syntax error?

```
for  x
```

```
        do
            echo $x
        done
```

No.

241. What is the difference between a hard and a soft link.

Hard link can not be used to link files in two different partitions and i-nodes of original and linked files are same. Whereas soft links can be made between files of different partitions.

242. What is the difference between a program and a process ? How can you find out processes started by you?

Process is a program under execution which can be uniquely identified by its stack pointer, program counter and PCB (process control block). By running ps command we can get process belongs to us.

243. Write a shell script which scans all C source programs in the directory (to be taken as first command line argument) and if C program uses the function name (to be taken as second command line argument) then compile the C program. If compilation is successful print the line

" OUTPUT OF THE program_name (to be substituted) " followed by the output of the C program.

Note : you may assume the given function is appearing only once in the program.

```
        cd $1
        for x in *.c
        if grep $2  $x >/dev/null
        then
            if  gcc $x >/dev/null
            then
                echo Output of $x
                $x
            fi
        fi
    done
```

244. What is the output of the following shell script.

```
for  x in .. .
   do
       ls $x
   done
```

Displays filenames in parent directory of P.W.D and files of P.W.D.

245. Write awk script to print the number of lines, number of words and number of characters in file1.

```
awk ' nw +=NF; nc += length($0)
END{ printf "Lines= %d\n Words=%d\nCharacters=%d\n", NR,nw,nc}'
filename
```

246. Write an awk script to copy the content of file1 to file2 after removing all blank lines.

```
awk ' $0 !~ /^$/ { print $0 }' file1 > file2
```

247. What does the following shell script do? Fill up the underlined portion of the message.

```
case $# in
    1) ; ;
    0) echo -------- exit ;;
esac
    if test ! -f $1
       then
           echo $0
           exit
       - 1>&2
               exit 3
    fi
```

If you run with no arguments if prints " -------" and exits. If you give one command line arguments then it tests whether it is a file or not. If it is a file it displays file name and exits.

248. A file contains two paragraphs (duplicates) only. What happens if you run uniq command on it?

Depends on the lines. If no two adjacent two lines of the paragraphs are same the all the lines of the file will be printed.

249. Design a pipe that sorts users presently working by login name.

who|sort

250. What the following command does?

grep rao raju | sort - rani > ROUT

Those lines of raju which contains rao and the lines of rani will be sorted alphabetically and result will be stored in ROUT.

251. How to make (for all the users) rm file to prompt before deleting a file

By putting alias rm 'rm -i' either in .cshrc of each user or in any global configuration file such as /etc/profile.

252. Write an alias command CD which immediately displays the path of your directory as soon as you change directory.

alias CD 'cd \!*; echo $cwd' where cwd built in shell variable which contains present working   directory name.

253. Setenv (without any arguments)   displays all environment variable information similarly , setenv TERM ______________

sets TERM value to null.

If you want to communicate a message through write, you should require write permissions from the other side. It is not so with mail.

254. What will happens if you run the following shell program with a file name as first argument.

```
file=$1
set `who am i`
mv $file $file.$1
```

Changes a specified file name such that its extension becomes its users name.

255. What is the output of the following shell script.

```
for  x in ..
do
     echo $x
done
```

Displays filenames in parent directory of P.W.D

256. Design a pipe that sorts by login name the list of people currently using the system.

```
who|sort
```

257. What the following command does ?

```
grep Rao Raju | sort - Rani >Rout
```

Those line of Raju which contains the Rao and the lines of file Rani will be stored in Rout in sorted order.

258. What will be the output of shell program (a) when executed with the following manners at the command prompt.

```
a -l 12 -b 22 -h 34
a -h 34 -b 22 -l 12
a -b 22 -h 34 -l 12
```

```
		for x in $*
		do
			case "$x" in

				-l) len=$2;
				  shift;;

				-b) breadth=$2;
				  shift;;

				-h) height=$2;
				  shift;;

			*) shift;;
			esac
		shift
		done
		echo "Volume=" `expr $len \* $breadth \* $height `
```

Displays volume as product of 22,34,12 with all the three manners.

259. **What will be the input for wc in the following command?.**
(who;date)|wc

output of both who and date commands.

260. **Explain why the following compound command hangs?**
(who;wc)|wc

wc command in parenthesis expects input from key board thus hangs.

261. **What is the difference between outputs of echo? and ls?**

echo? displays filenames (single character length) of P.W.D. ls ? displays filenames (single character length) of P.W.D and sub directories in it.

262. **What happens if you execute the following command?**
cat b >> b

error message **Input is same as output** will appear. However, b file content will be same.

263. **What happens if you execute the following command?.**
cat b > b

error message **Input is same as output** will appear. However, b file content will be lost.

264. **What will be the output of the following command?.**
wc b c

Total no of lines, words, characters of files b and c and will be displayed.

265. **What will be the output of the following command?.**
wc b > b

File b after the command contains " 0 0 0 b". Reason is, when you say >b its content will be first wiped out then on that wc is executed.

266. **What happens if you run the following command?.**
wc b >>b

How many lines, word, characters are there in the file b will be appended to b itself.

267. **Does uniq command can be used remove multiple blank lines s in the given file.**

No

268. **Explain what happens**

(a)	echo *	Displays all entries of P.W.D
(b)	echo **	Displays all entries of P.W.D
(c)	echo *:*	Displays * : *
(d)	echo `*`	Error
(e)	echo '*'	Displays *
(f)	echo '**'	Displays **
(g)	echo `**`	Error
(h)	echo "**"	Displays **
(i)	echo "*"	Displays *

269. Differentiate between

        ls   *   verses   echo *

Both displays entries of P.W.D. However, ls * displays content of sub-directories also.

        ls *t* verses echo *t*
        same as above explanation

270. Differentiate between

        ls ? vs echo ?

same as above explanation

271. Differentiate between

        rm ch* vs rm ch *

Second one is more dangerous than the first one which removes file ch and all files whereas the first one removes only those files which starts with ch.

272. What is the difference

        cc a.c b.c
        and
        cc A.c

where a.c and b.c contents are in A.c

In reality no difference. However, two separate object files will be created.

273. What is the use of cxref?.

        generates cross-reference listing of a C program.

274. What happens if you run the following shell script

        for f in *.c
          do
            admin -n i$f s.$f
          done

This would place all c language file in P.W.D under sccs.

275. **What will be the output of the following command ?**
sort -t: +3 /etc/passwd

Sorts the file /etc/passwd based on fourth field on words

276. **What will be the action of the following command?.**
sed '/^$/ d' filename

deletes all the empty lines.

277. **What will be the value of N if you execute the following commands on xyz file?.**

N1=`wc -l xyz`
N2=`sed '/^$/ d' xyz | wc -l`
N = `expr $N1 - $N2`

Number of empty lines in the file xyz.

278. **In the following command**
sed -n '/pqr/ s/xyz/XYZ/gp' filename
Replaces all occurrences of xyz in lines which contains pqr and prints only changed lines.

279. **What will be the output of the following command ?**
sed -n '/^$/ p' filename
Displays all lines of the file which are not empty lines.

280. **What will be the output of following shell script?**

N1= `sed  -n  '/^$/ p'  filename`
N2= `sed  -n  '/^$/ !p'  filename`
echo `expr $N2 + $N1 `

Total number of lines in the given file.

281. **What will be the output of following command on file abc containing xyz pattern in many lines.**

sed -n '/xyz/ !p' abc

Displays those lines of the file abc which does not contain search word xyz.

282. In the sed command what n option does ?

sed '/^\\begin\(sec/ n' a.tex

Display those lines of the a.tex which comes after a line which starts with pattern \begin(sec.

283. A database file consists first field as name and second field as telephone numbers along with area code (0891-553471). Write a shell command which display telephone numbers sorted (without local code).

cut -f2 filename |cut -d "-" -f2|sort

284. A database file consists first field as name and second field as telephone numbers along with area (0891-553471) Write a shell program which display telephone numbers which are not in use.

```
I=1
for x in `cut -f2 filename |cut -d"-" -f2|sort`
 do
   if [ $I -eq 1 ]
   then
     MIN=$x
     I=2
     else
         MAX=$x
        J=`expr $MIN + 1`
        while [ $J -lt $MAX ]
          do
            echo $J
            J=`expr $J + 1`
          done
        MIN=$MAX
     fi
 done
```

285. Explain what happens the following korn shell program does?.

```
if test -G $1
  then
      echo you are owner
else
    echo who are you guy\?
fi
```

If the owner file runs then first echo statement will be executed otherwise the second one will be executed.

286. What happens if you execute the following command

echo Enter $amount or * to see all the customers.

Displays the following:

Enter followed by value of amount and names of all the files in P.W.D and to see all the customers.

287. echo $? displays exit status of previous command in Bourne shell. Which command is used for the same in C shell?.

echo $status.

288. In korn shell what will be the output of following sequence of commands.

```
xyz[0]=Ram
xyz[1]=Ravi
xyz[10]=Raju
echo xyz[*]
echo ${#xyz[*]}
```

Last statement displays 11 (no of elements in xyz)
Last but one statement displays Ram, Ravi, Raju.

289. **A file is having place names, population, country in each record, write an awk command to display those records which belongs to INDIA?.**

awk '$3 ~ /INDIA/' filename (default field separator is assumed).

290. **What does the following awk statement will do?.**

awk '($0 ~ /^$/) && ($1 > 100) { print $0}' filename

Displays those records which are not blank and the first field value is greater than 100.

291. **What will be the output of following awk command?.**

awk 'BEGIN{print "FILENAME", FILENAME}
END{print "No. Of Records", NR}' file1 file2   file3

FILENAME
No of Records 21 (some no)

292. **What will be the output if you run the following awk script?.**

awk 'BEGIN{pline=""}
     {
     if ($0 != pline) {print $0}}
     {pline=$0}' filename

Displays uniq lines. That is if there are two or more lines which are same, this prints only one for all.

293. **What should be the umask value such that others are out of any new file created by you?.**

027

294. **What does the following command does?.**
sort +0.2 -0.8 filename

sorts the file based on 2 to 8 characters.

295. What the following command does in C shell?.

   set month=`date + '%m'`

       month variable value becomes current month.

296. What is the equivalent command in sed for the command line<filename?.

       sed -e `-2,$d' filename

297. Write an equivalent shell script using cut, paste for the following awk command:

   awk -F: '{print $5 $1}' /etc/passwd


```
cut -f1 -d: /etc/passwd > x1
cut -f5 -d: /etc/passwd > x2
paste x1 x2
```

298. A students id, name, marks in five tests are available in file (stud) with field separator |. Write an awk program to display a table containing id, name, and class. (Joke : Assuming no need to pass in each test !!!).

```
awk –F| '{
        avg=($3+$4+$5+$6+$7)/5
        if(avg >= 60) {grade="First Class"}
        if((avg >= 50) && (avg <60)) {grade="Second Class"}
        if((avg >= 35) && (avg <50)) {grade="Third Class"}
        if(avg < 35) {grade="Failed"}

        }
        { print $1 $2 grade }' stud
```

299. Repeat on the above data file (stud) and write shell program with awk to display identification number of those student who got class first.

```
awk –F| '{sum=$3+$4+$5+$6+$7
        if (sum >= 60) {print $1}} ' stud
```

300. Repeat on the above data file (stud) and write awk program which displays id, CGPA (central grade point average) where 10, 8, 6, 4, 2 points are given if marks in a test are greater than or equal to 80, 60, 40, 20, and 0 respectively.

```
awk –F| '{ s=0
        for(i=3;i<=7;i++)
         { s=s+2*(5-(4-$i/20))}
        s=s/5
        }
        {
        print $1, $2,s}' stud
```

301. Repeat on the above data file (stud) and write an awk program to display grades in each test and overall CGPA for each student.

```
awk –F| 'BEGIN{
        G[5]="A"
        G[4]="B"
        G[3]="C"
        G[2]="D"
        G[1]="E"
        }
        {
        s=0
          {
           print $1 $2
          }
        for(i=3;i<=7;i++)
        {
        p=(5-(4-$i/20))
        s=s+2*p
          {
           print $i G[p]
          }
        }
        s=s/5
        }
        {print s}' stud
```

302. A data file of a telephone department consists of name, number, dues fields and an attribute field which contains either of the following words: normal, retired, political, transfer, departmental, pending. Write a program which displays total amount in each of the categories.

```
awk -F"|" ' BEGIN{
            categ["Normal"]=0
            categ["retired"]=0
            categ["political"]=0
            categ["transfer"]=0
            categ["departmental"]=0
            categ["pending"]=0
            }
        SUM[$4]+=$3
      END{
    for(x in categ)
       {print x, SUM[x]}}'  file
```

303. Write an awk script which displays whether a specified file is having exactly same size (in number of characters) records or not?.

```
awk 'BEGIN{ANS=0}
  {
  if (ANS == 0 )
    {
      LL=length($0)
      ANS=1
    }
  else
    {
    if (LL != length($0)) {
                ANS=0
                exit
                }
```

```
                    }

              }
              END{
                  if (ANS == 0) {print "NO"}

                  else

                  {print "YES"}

                  }' filename
```

304. **If a variable is not defined then what will be the result if you use test command with that variable ?.**

returns false.

305. **What will be action of following command?**

echo f1 f2 >> tmp

where f1, f2 and tmp are files.

The string f1 f2 will be appended to the file tmp.

306. **Why sticky bit is not available in recent UNIX systems?.**

Because present systems uses demand paging.

307. **What will be the action of the following command.**

rsh rambha cat /etc/motd > temp

/etc/motd file on machine rambha is copied to file temp on local machine.

308. **Are there any UNIX commands that take input directly from user without intervention of shell?.**

Yes. Examples vi, adb etc.

309. **What is the output of the following shell script.**

```
for  x in
    do
        echo $x
    done
```

Displays nothing.

310. **If you want to change ownership and group of one of your file then which command you have to execute first?. Why?**

chgrp. If you change ownership first then you don't have privilege to change group later as you are no longer owner!.

311. **Write a single command line statement (using redirection, pipes, and tees) that will accept lines typed through the keyboard and copy them in sorted order in a file "xyz" and will also count the number of lines and store the count in another file "xyz1".**

```
cat -|tee xyz|wc -l >xyz1
```

312. **Write a shell script which will execute the cp program as a child process. Clearly identify how many arguments are necessary for simple copy.**

The shell script should contains
```
cp $1 $2
```

313. **Write a while statement that performs the following code:**

```
while (number of arguments on the command line not equal to zero)
    display the first argument
```

```
        dispose of the first argument
        end of while

    while [ $# -gt 0 ]
      do
       echo $1
       shift
      done
```

314. Write a simple Bourne for structure that displays all of the arguments on the command line.

```
    for  x in $*
    do
    echo $x
    done
```

315. Give the command line command that executes the previous command.

```
      !!
```

316. Write single command which lists only sub-directory names.

```
    ls -l|grep "^d"|awk '{print $9}'
```

317. Write a piping command which displays c program file names and file sizes of files in P.W.D.

```
    ls -l *.c|grep "^-" |awk '{printf " %s  %7d\n", $9, $5}'|more
```

318. A file contains names, designation and employee number. Write awk program to display names of people whose employee number is between 520 and 540. (Fields are separated by | symbol)

```
    awk -F"|" ' $3>=520 && $3<=540 {print $1}'  filename
```

319. Write a program to print c language file names whose file sizes are between 500 and 1000 bytes of P.W.D.

```
    ls -l *.c|grep "^-" |awk ' $5 >=500 && $5<= 1000 { print $9}'
```

320. Write a program which displays 5'th line of a file.

```
head -5 filename|tail -1
```

321. Write a shell script which takes a string displays it and continues taking characters till you press enter without a character.

```
echo "Enter a string"
read ss
echo $ss
x=
while [ "$x" != "$ss" ]
do
read ss
done
```

322. Write a shell script which check for core file in your directory at regular intervals (interval time is specified along the command line) and removes the same.

```
while ls core 2>/dev/null
do
rm core
sleep $1
done
```

323. Write a shell program which removes those files of C.W.D whose sizes are more than 1K.

```
p=ls –l– awk –F"|" ' $5>1000 {print $9}'`
echo $9
for x in 9
do
rm $x
done
```

324. Write a shell script which prints total files size of P.W.D.

```
ls -l|grep "^-"|awk ' s+=$5
END{printf "%d" s}'
```

325. Write a shell script which takes a command line argument (a command name) and displays in which directory of $PATH, this command's machine languages file is available. If number of command line arguments are zero print an error.

```
if [ $# -eq 1 ]
then
IFS=:
for x in $PATH
do
if ls $x/$1 1> /dev/null 2>&1
 then
 echo found
 exit
 fi
done
echo Not found
else
echo Not sufficient number of arguments
fi
```

326. What will be the result of the following shell script.

```
IFS=:
for x in $PATH
do
echo $x
done
```

Displays directory names in $PATH variable in one line each.

327. Does the following two programs work in similar manner

```
IFS=:
for x in $PATH
do
```

```
echo $x
done
```

```
IFS=:
for x in "$PATH"
do
echo $x
done
```

```
 No.
First one gives the following results.
/usr/local/bin
/bin
/usr/bin
/usr/X11/bin
/usr/andrew/bin
/usr/openwin/bin
/usr/games

.
```

```
Second one gives the following results.
/usr/local/bin /bin /usr/bin /usr/X11/bin /usr/andrew/bin /usr/openwin/bin
/usr/games.
```

328. Does the following programs does work similarly

```
IFS=:
for x in $PATH
do
echo $x
done
```

```
IFS=" "
H=`echo $PATH|awk -F":" '{print $0}`
for x in $H
```

```
    do
    echo $x
    done
```

Ans: No

329. If v is a shell script and if you run the following command what will be the output?

```
v>>v
```

text file busy

330. A entry given in the following entry displays

```
who::65535:65535:who command:/:/bin/who
```

Displays who are logged in on the system.

331. What will be the output of the following command?.

```
ls|(wc >xyz 2 > /dev/null) 2>&1
```

332. In C shell what does the following command does?.

```
(wc <xyz >mno) > error
```

Standard error will be written in file error and output in mno.

333. In the following command commands in parenthesis will be executed in present shell or sub-shell?.

```
(wc <xyz >mno) > eror
```

sub-shell.

334. Size /bin/vi command displayed the following. Explain what does each item explain.

Text   data   bss   dec   hex

98304   8192   39032   145528   23879

vi has 98304 instructions

 8192 bytes of data

39032 symbols and strings

145528 total bytes.

23879 total bytes in hexadecimal.

335. What happens if lex specification file contains an empty line in its definitions section.

Generates a C source program which takes standard input and displays the same onto standard output without any modifications.

336. /etc/services file contains the following information. Explain what is the meaning of them?.

finger 79/TCP

sunrpc 111/TCP

First field indicates service type, second filed number indicates port number and other indicates protocol used.

337. What option with ls command to print comma separated list?.

-m

338. What will be the output of

find /home/venkat -type b -perm 0002 -print

Displays those files of /home/venkat which has world writable permissions.

339. **With find command what is the difference between the following options**

      -perm 0002

      -perm -0002

If hyphen is there then it will display the file permissions are set in the given mask. Whereas the other reports exact match.

340. **What will be the output of**

      find. -type f -links +1 -print

341. **Two files can be merged together vertically using the command at the command line.**

      paste

342. **What will be the output of the following C shell script?.**

```
foreach dir ( $path )
  if ( -x $dir/gcc ) then
     echo Found $dir/gcc
     break
  else
     echo Searching $dir/gcc
  endif
end
```

It checks for the executable file 'gcc' in all directories in path variable if it is found in any one it will display else it will display a message saying searching.

343. **What is the use of acl?.**

access control in some recent UNIX systems.

344. **What is the use of rmcr in some UNIX systems?.**

To remove carriage return from files especially DOS files.

345. Presently noclabber is set and want to redirect the output of a command 'x 'to an existing file xyz what command should be executed?

x>!xyz

346. What is the use of script?.

To record entire shell session what commands are executed and their output.

347. To suspend a process (PID=222) ctrl z will be used what is its equivalent through kill?.

kill -18 222

348. What is the equivalent Bourne shell program for the following C shell program.

```
foreach name ( $argv )
    echo Saying hello to $name
    echo "Hello from $user " | write $name
end
```

```
for name in $*
    do
        echo "Saying hello to $name"
        echo "Hello from $USER"|write $name
    done
```

349. What is the meaning of $< in the following script?.

```
switch ( $< )
case y: breaksw
default: echo "Doing nothing!" exit 0
endsw
```

To get a line from user

350. Why .login file is not important on those systems such as Xterminals and X servers?.

As X uses its own login procedure.

351. Does .login is executed when you execute a sub-shell?.

No. It is used by login shell only.

352. What is the output of the following command?.

    alias dir 'ls -lg \!* | more'

    Error

353. What happens if the `breaksw' commands are omitted with a case statement in C shell?.

Control flows through all the commands following it.

354. What is the meaning if =~ test condition is used with if statement in C Shell.

Matches a wildcard

355. The following C shell example displays Shutdown time...' five times at 30 second intervals, before shutting down the system. What is its equivalent in Bourne shell.

repeat 5 echo `echo "Shutdown time! Log out now" | wall ; sleep 30`

356. What is the difference between break and breaksw in C shell.

    break breaks loops whereas breaksw breaks switch statement.

357. If x = /home/venkat/nbv.c then what option can be used to display only path of the file nbv.c?.

    :h

Example : echo $x:h

358. Write a script to read a set of strings till you enter quit. If you press CTRL D in between it should display exiting.

```
echo "Enter words"
while read word
do
if [ "$word" = "quit" ]
 then
      echo "(So I quit!)"
       exit 0
fi
done
echo "exiting"
```

359. Explain the difference between shared library and static library?.

Usually static libraries will have extension .a whereas the shared will have.so or.sa. When an static library is linked to a program, it is appended to the program code. This uses a lot of disk space and makes the size of the compiled program very large. Whereas with Shared libraries the code is not appended to the program. Instead pointers to the shared objects are created and the library is loaded at runtime, thus avoiding the problem of having to store the library effectively multiple times on the disk.

360. What is the use of ldconfig command?.

To add shared library path to LD_LIBRARY_PATH.

361. How to stop passing an environment variable to a sub-shell in a shell script.

```
unset it near the top of your script.
```

362. What is the difference between $* and $@?.

They behave differently when they occur inside double quotes.

363. What is the difference between the following shell scripts?

(a)

```
for X in "$*"
    do
```

```
                echo $X
        done
```

(b)

```
        for X in "$@"
            do
                echo $X
        done
```

364. How can you make a dash also a character with pattern matching?.

[-q] which will match either a dash or q.

365. What is the meaning of <&- ?

Close standard input.

366. Why commands in initialization files such as /etc/profile are sourced rather than executed?.

These commands should change the environment of current shell.

367. Presently PWD is /home/guest1. What will be the results of echo `pwd` command after executing the following shell script which contains single line cd /tmp?.

/home/guest1

368. What is the use of ENV environment variable?.

ENV points to a file which is to be sourced whenever a new *interactive* shell is started.

369. What will be output of the following command sequence?.

env | wc -c

Displays amount memory (in bytes) used by the environment in the current shell process.

370. What is the effect of the following command?.

       set -o trackall

The shell "tracks" all aliased commands. That is, it "remembers" where an executable file was found, and won't search PATH again for it if it is still valid. (not available in bash)

371. What is the use of ulimit command?.

Ulimit is usually a shell built-in. It sets process limits, controlling such things as maximum file size, maximum size core dumps, whether core dumps should be produced at all, etc. Limits set in a start-up file apply to your login shell, and all processes it spawns. We can see the values currently in effect with ulimit -a.

372. What is the meaning of the following command?.

       cmd > out.txt 2>&1 &

standard out but of cmd and standard error are redirected to out.txt and whole command will be executed in background.

373. How do I remove a file whose name begins with a "-" ?

       rm ./\-filename

374. What is the use of getopt() function?.

This function is used to parse command line arguments

375. If one wants to make a directory as unsearchable what permissions has to be given for it.

       chmod a-x directoryname

376. What does the following command does?.

       find . -inum 12354 -ok rm '{}' \;

removes file in the PWD (or in its subdirectories) whose i-node number is 12354.

377. **Which are the characters that can not appear in filenames theoretically?.**

'/' and '\0'

378. **Which character is available at the end of a filename?.**

'\0'

379. **Which command is used to clear i-node information?.**

clri

380. **What is the effect of the following command (C Shell).**

```
alias setprompt 'set prompt="${cwd}% "'
setprompt
alias cd 'chdir \!* && setprompt'
```

whenever you change directory its path will be visible in the prompt.

381. **What is the meaning of %/   in tcsh?.**

the full pathname of the current directory

382. **Write a shell program in sh to read a character.**

```
echo -n "Enter a character: "
stty cbreak       # or  stty raw
readchar=`dd if=/dev/tty bs=1 count=1 2>/dev/null`
stty -cbreak

echo "Thank you for typing a $readchar ."
```

383. **What is the out of the following command in Bourne shell?.**

```
for f in *
```

```
        do
          mv $f `echo $f | tr '[A-Z]' '[a-z]'`
        done
```

changes file names of PWD to upper to lower.

384. Write an awk script to calculate the average number of words per line in given file FILE.

```
awk 's +=NF END{printf "%d", s/NR} ' FILE
```

385. Write awk script which calculates the sum of n (to be taken as command line argument) columns for each record and at the end prints grand total.

```
awk ' n='$1' { s=0
         for(i=1;i<=n;i++)
            s += $i
         printf "ROW=%d, SUM=%d\n",NR, s
            t += s
            } END{ printf "Grand Total=%d\n", t } ' FILE
```

386. Write a shell script which calculates number of empty lines in a file FILE.

```
N = 0
while read line
do
if [ "$line" = "" ]
then
 N=`expr $N + 1`
fi
done<FILE
echo $N
```

387. Write a shell script which takes a command line argument of kilometers and by default converts that number to meters. Also provide -d option to convert kilometers to decimeters and -c option to convert to centimeters.

```
        case "$1" in
         -d) echo `expr $2 \* 10000 `
            ;;
         -c) echo `expr $2 \* 100000 `
            ;;
         -*) echo `expr $1 \* 1000 `
            ;;
        esac
```

Typical usage assuming CONV is the shell program name

```
    CONV 7
    CONV -c 7
    CONV -d 7
```

388. Instead of the usual printf(format, parameter) command, need a printf(x,y,format,parameter) command where x and y are screen coordinates in shell.

```
have a shell script with the following lines
    # usage: PRINTF text row column
    tput cup $2 $3
    echo "$1"
```

389. Which option can be used with tar to extract the files in it?

```
xf or –xf
```

390. Which option can be used with tar to display the files in it?

```
-t
```

391. Which daemon manages network related aspects?

```
inetd (Also called as super server)
```

392. Which command can be used to split large text files?

```
split
```

393. Which account is created when Linux is installed?

root

394. What are the commands related to shadow password management?

pwconv, pwunconv, grpconv, grpunconv.

395. What is the use of repquota command?

Displays details about disk usage.

396. Which mode the file system has to be mounted for checking file system in consistency?

readonly

397. Which command is used to find what a given command does?

whatis

398. Which commands can be used to change permissions of a running process?

top, nice

399. Which is the command to change run levels?

init

400. kill 0 commands kills all process. Is it true?

No. It will not kill login shell.

401. How does files, directories, devices are recognized by the UNIX kernel?

Based on first 4 bits of mode bits.

402. What scheduling is employed in Linux?

For the conventional time –shared processes, Linux uses a prioritized, credit-based algorithm. Each process possesses a certain number of scheduling credits; when a new task must be chosen to run, the process with most credits is selected. Every time that a timer interrupt occurs, the currently running process loses one credit; when its credits reaches zero, it is suspended and another process is chosen. If no runnable processes have any credits, then Linux performs a re-crediting operation, adding credits to every process in the system (rather than just to the runnable ones), according to the following rule:

$$Credits = credits/2 + priority$$

The above scheduling class is used for time-shared process and the in Linux for the real-time scheduling is simpler it uses scheduling classes: first come, first served (FCFS), and round-robin (RR) .In both cases, each process has a priority in addition to its scheduling class. In time-sharing scheduling, however, processes of different priorities can still compete with one another to some extent; in real-time scheduling, the scheduler always runs the process with the highest priority. Among processes of equal priority, it runs the process that has been waiting longest. The only difference between FCFS and RR scheduling is that FCFS processes continue to run until they either exit or block, whereas a round-robin process will be preempted after a while and will be moved to the end of the scheduling queue, so round-robin processes of equal priority will automatically time share among themselves. Linux's real-time scheduling is soft-real time rather than hard-real time. The scheduler offers strict guarantees about the relative priorities of real-time processes, but the kernel does not offer any guarantees about how quickly a real-time process will be scheduled once that process becomes runnable. Thus the Linux uses different scheduling classes for time-shared and real-time processes

403. What is the use of dmesg command?

To see the bootup time messages.

404. What is the minimum swap partition size needed for Linux.

16MB. However it is recommended to have two times of RAM for desktop machines. But for servers, there is no rule of thumb. We can create swap files also as and when red.

405. What is the out put of shell script.

```
$7=you
$8=are
$9=good
    echo $7 $8 $9
```

Error

406. What is the use of the following command?

Kill 0

Kills all processes except login shell.

407. How to switch to super user status to gain priveleges?

Use su command

408. How many prompts are there in UNIX?

Four prompts PS1, PS2, PS3 and PS4. They may vary from shell to shell.

409. What is the difference between lilo/stub?

lilo is Linux boot loades.

Stub is a temporary implementation of w part of a program for debugging purpose.

410. What commands are related to shell's job control?

fg and bg

411. What are windows equivalent of UNIX Daemons?

Background service processes or service agents.

412. What is kernal?

The kernal is part of OS that interacts daily with HW of the computer.

413. What is the command that can be used to find the location of the command to be run?

which

Example

which ls

414. We have to find a command say xyz in /bin but do not know what for it. How to break this barrier?

What is command can be used.

Ex

What is   xyz

What is   ls

415. What is the utility to show dynamic listing of running processes?

top

416. Which is the dacmon responsible for tracking events on our Linux System?

syslogd

417. What is the effect of the following command?
set −o vi

sets vi as our command line editor

418. Can we mount root partition as read write mode during fsck?

No.

419. What is the use of pwconv command?

To improve system security by (creating /etc/shadow file.

420. What is the use of kmem group in /etc/group file?

Kmem group manages direct access yp kernal memory.

421. Is it possible to change priority of a process using top utility?

Yes.

422. What is the name of system file which defines levels of messages that are written to system log?

Kernel. w

423. If two files exists with same I-node in two different directories, what do you say about them?

They are hard-link files.

424. **Which command can be used to remove password of a group?**

gpasswd –r

425. **Why do we need password for a group?**

Guess?

426. **We have a file with unequal length lines. We want to bring all of them to same length. Which command can be used?**

fmt

427. **Which command can be used to find what SHELL we are using?**

echo $SHELL

428. **Which command can be used to prepare boot disk under Linux distributions?**

mkbootdisk

429. **Does ipchains settings will be saved during reboot or shutdown?**

No.

430. **Which package can be used to regulate the TCP/IP network traffic?**

tcp–wrappers

431. **For a mail server (exclusive for mail services) which partition is crucial?**

/var/spool

432. **What type of server is needed to remotely assign IP addresses to m/c's during the installation processes?**

DHCP

433. In which directory and its sub-directories system configuration files are located?

/etc

434. What is the use of logrotate and prerotate?

They are bash script utilities to manage, archive log files.

435. What is the response of the following command?

cat   xyz   & > abc

It redirects both standard output and error to a file.

436. During Linux booting we have got LIL and system hanged. Why?

First and second stages of LILO is completed. However, map file could not get loaded. May be media failure.

437. Which configuration file defines which start up scripts to run at each run level?

/etc/inittab

438. Which configuration file is used to pass parameters to loadable modules?

/etc/conf.modules

439. How to add new group with some users?

edit /etc/group file

440. How to give freedom to users to mount Hoppy?

Edit the /etc/fstab file and add the user options to floppy entry.

441. How to suspend a running procets and out it in background?

By pressing ctrl + z

442. Which commands can be used to run a program at a specified time on a specified day?

at and crontab

443. **The following entry is used in /etc/passwd file. Does the user rao can login**
     rao : jumbo : 504 : 101: rao PN : /home/rao:/bin/bash

No.

444. **As a superuser can we edit /etc/passwd file to give password to a user?**

No.

445. **Which command can be used to copy the superblock to the first block of**
     partition?

e2fsck

446. **What file we need to change to alter how the updatedb database is**
     created?

/etc/updatedb.conf

447. **Which file can be modified to change window manager?**

.xinitrc

448. **Is chps is a valid UNIX command?**

No.

449. **What happens it you run mount command with out any arguments?**

Displays all mounted partitions and information is taken from /etc/fstab file

450. **As an administrator you have added new shell scripts to systems under**
     /home/shell. You want all the users of your system to use them without
     typing the commands (scripts) path. Which file do you need to modify?

/etc/profile

451. **Which log file can be used to know which users did not login in the last**
     three months?

/var/log/last log

452. If we keep * at the beginning of password field of an account what happens to that user?

He can not log in

453. How to change system run level?

init runlevelnumber

454. What is single user mode?

Linux will be in single user mode during starting. It runs /bin/su and log's in as root and.

455. With which command we can update what is database?

makewhatis

456. Does find command uses what is database?

No.

457. Both what is and find commands works in same fashion?

No.

458. df /home command output is

Amount of disk space used by /home and free space available.

459. What is the effect of the following command?

dd if=/dev/fdo   bs=512   of=/new

If copies contents of floppy to file /new.

460. Which directory is used to store process related information?

/proc

461. How to test lilo modifications without installing the same?

LILO –t

462. What is the effect of head *. command

Display ten lines of all files of C.W.D

463. I have a file with TAB separated entries. How to change TABS to single spaces.

expand –t1 filename

464. How can I shutdown Linux machine cleanly ?

reboot

shutdown –r

init   6

465. Which text files can be used to see a file content in octal?

od

Multiple Choice Questions

1. Find **odd-man** out of the following
   (a) sed
   (b) ed
   (c) tr
   (d) grep

2. The objective of a **time-sharing** operating system is to
   (a) minimize the net execution time
   (b) maximize processor utilization
   (c) minimize the user response time
   (d) none of the above

3. In UNIX terminology, a **process** is a
   (a) program in execution
   (b) subprogram which can be called from other program
   (c) sequence of commands which are in order
   (d) none

4. **Fork** system call
   (a) splits a process
   (b) creates another copy of the process which calls fork and executes concurrently.
   (c) change the standard output to other device
   (d) none

5. UNIX **system calls** are to
   (a) request for service(s) offered by the OS kernel
   (b) a mechanism using which one program can call another
   (c) a signal generated by the OS signaling an error
   (d) none

6. If **x** is a program then **x\&** at command prompt
   (a) executes x background
   (b) x executes with highest priority
   (c) executes only when other programs are not working
   (d) none

7. In UNIX, **mounting a file system** means
   (a) copying all the files from one file system to another
   (b) moving all the files from one file system to another
   (c) loading a file system from backup medium like tape
   (d) providing a link to the file system to be mounted so that it appears as a local device.

8. Proper **shutdown** procedure is required in UNIX
   (a) otherwise the file system may become inconsistent
   (b) all users must be informed that the system is being switched off
   (c) the power to the disk and display units must be shutoff first
   (d) none

9. Which of the following things are true about **symbolic links**?.
   (a) can be made to a directory
   (b) the file can be accessed through the symbolic link even after the original file has been deleted.
   (c) the creation of each symbolic link causes the link count to be incremented
   (d) none

10. The file **/usr/lib/crontab** is handy place to put files that are to be run
   (a) at the highest execution priority
   (b) each time a user logs out of the system
   (c) each time a user logs out of system
   (d) none

11. **Information** about **a file** is stored in
   (a) a system-wide file table
   (b) the i-node associated with the file
   (c) a file allocation table within the kernel
   (d) none

12. The UNIX **system calls** are used to
   (a) inform the system administrator about an abnormal situation.
   (b) obtain some service from the kernel
   (c) execute a UNIX command from a shell script
   (d) none

13. The command to **copy a file from remote machine to local** machine through ftp is
   (a) get   (b) rep
   (c) copy   (d) bring

14. In UNIX the **free data blocks** are arranged in
   (a) linked list   (b) array
   (c) sequentially   (d) none

15. To **convert UNIX** OS text file to **DOS** format the command is
   (a) unixtodos   (b) unix_to_dos
   (c) unixdos   (d) udos

16. Command which **informs the user automatically about arrival of a new mail**
   (a) mailcheck   (b) notify
   (c) rmail   (d) mailx

17. The program which takes user input, **interprets** it and takes necessary actions
   (a) kernel   (b) system calls
   (c) shell   (d) scheduler

18. Its main job is to **allocate CPU to process**
   (a) login   (b) shell
   (c) getty   (d) scheduler

19. What is the output of the following command in the **C shell**
     set a = (hello my dear appu)
     echo $a[1]$a[3-]
     (a)   hello my dear appu   (b)   hello my dear
     (c)   hellodear appu   (d)   none

20. In which shell you can think a **shell variable as an array**.
     (a)   ksh   (b)   csh
     (c)   bash   (d)   all

21. What is the output of the following command in C shell.
     set X=(I am too much fond of my dear Appu); echo $#X
     (a)   I am too much fond of my dear Appu
     (b)   error
     (c)   9
     (d)   none

22. **Switch** construct is used in
     (a)   c language   (b)   bash
     (c)   Berkeley C shell   (d)   a & c

23. In which shell, directory **stack** is available ?.
     (a)   korn   (b)   Bourne
     (c)   Berkeley C   (d)   none

24. If you execute the following command in C shell **what is the output.**
     set p=(cls cd P.W.D who); echo $p[$#p]
     (a)   who   (b)   list of users
     (c)   ls cd P.W.D who   (d)   none

25. What is the output of the following command.
     set history = 100; set p = (ls P.W.D cd who); echo `$p[$#p]`
     (a)   ls P.W.D cd who
     (b)   who
     (c)   details of the users working at that time
     (d)   none

26. What is the output of the following command.
     set p = (ls pwd cd who); echo `$p[-$#p]` this command gives
     (a)   ls P.W.D cd who
     (b)   who
     (c)   tries to list file names P.W.D, cd and who and as they are not available you get
           error message.
     (d)   none

27. What is the output of the following command
     set p = (ls P.W.D cd who); set p[3] = hello; echo $p
     (a)   ls P.W.D cd who   (b)   who
     (c)   ls P.W.D hello who   (d)   none

28. What is the output of the following command.
     set p=(ls P.W.D cd who); set p[3]="how are"; echo $p
     (a)   ls P.W.D cd who
     (b)   ls P.W.D how who
     (c)   ls P.W.D how are who
     (d)   syntax error, sorry one word can not be replaced with two.

29. What is the output of the following command.
     set p = (ls P.W.D cd who); set p[3] = "how are"; echo $#p
     (a)   5   (b)   ls P.W.D cd who
     (c)   4   (d)   ls P.W.D how are who

30. What is the output of the following command.
     set p = (cd P.W.D who how); set p[3] = "ls –l"; echo `$p[3]`
     (a)   syntax error
     (b)   lists how directory listing
     (c)   lists present directory listing in long fashion
     (d)   none

31. What is the output of the following command.
     set p = (cd P.W.D who /tmp); set p[3] = "ls – l"; echo`$p[3-]`
     (a)   syntax error   (b)   directory listing of /tmp
     (c)   cd P.W.D ls-l /tmp   (d)   none

32. What is the output of the following command.
     set p = (cd ls who /tmp); set p[2] = "ls -l"; echo`$p[2]  $p[$#p]`
     (a)   syntax error   (b)   lists directory in for /tmp
     (c)   cd P.W.D ls-l /tmp   (d)   none

33. What happens if you run **set time = 0** in **C shell**
     (a)   time will be initiated to zero
     (b)   a times is started
     (c)   for every command execution times will be displayed
     (d)   none

34. When **i-nodes** are created ? ___________.
     (a)   boot time   (b)   when file system is created
     (c)   manufacturing time   (d)   none.

35. **System Executable** files for system administration are in
     (a)   /bin   (b)   /sbin
     (c)   /tmp   (d)   none

36. Which are the shell **setup files** (**C shell**) normally users can use.
     (a)   .profile   (b)   .cshrc
     (c)   .login,.logout   (d)   b & c.

37. What is equivalent commands in **Bourne shell** for
     setenv PATH /bin:/user/bin:.:$HOME/bin
     (a)   PATH = /bin:/user/bin:.:$HOME/bin
     (b)   set path = (/bin /user/bin. ~/bin)
     (c)   set PATH = (. $HOME/bin /bin /usr/bin)
     (d)   none

38. Which of the following commands work
     1. cat food 2>&1 >file
     2. cat food >file 2>&1
     (a)   1   (b)   2
     (c)   1 & 2   (d)   none

39. What is the output of the following script if executed at command line.
     WISH="HI, $USER
     >Good Morning
     >The Date and Time
     > are :`date`"
     echo "$WISH"
     (a)   Hi, jerry, Good Morning, The date and Time are: The sep 13 13:48:12.
     (b)   Hi, jerry, Good Morning The date and Time are The sep 13 13
     (c)   error
     (d)   none

40. **cat -v .** produces
     (a)   List of file names starting with. (dot).
     (b)   List of filenames in P.W.D.
     (c)   displays all files in P.W.D.
     (d)   error

41. What will be the **optional buffer size** while doing I/O operations on disk.
     (a)   2k
     (b)   512
     (c)   1k
     (d)   largest physical record the I/O channel is likely required to handle.

42. **Iscntrl** function returns true if it its arguments value is
     (a)   alphabets   (b)   octal 0 to 37
     (c)   127   (d)   b & c

43. What will be the output of **echo *.**
     (a)   *.   (b)   all files content.
     (c)   names of files in P.W.D excluding (d)   all dot files. Dot files.

44. What will be the output of **echo .***
     (a)   .*.   (b)   all files with extension.
     (c)   .,.., dot file names in P.W.D. (d)   all dot files content.

45. tee command __________.
    (a) can break pipe
    (b) behaves like cd command in pipe.
    (c) allows to write standard output of previous command in pipe to a file and simultaneously it gives standard output.
    (d) a & b

46. Any thing **between single quotes** __________ by shell.
    (a) leaves it alone
    (b) process
    (c) expanded
    (d) none of the above

47. **touch** and **cat** are
    (a) to create files
    (b) touch creates only empty file
    (c) both
    (d) none

48. **Commands between parenthesis will be executed** in
    (a) current
    (b) background
    (c) sub-shell
    (d) none

49. **Commands between curly braces** will be executed in
    (a) current shell
    (b) back ground
    (c) sub-shell
    (d) none

50. **Commands between back quotes** will be executed in
    (a) background
    (b) sub-shell
    (c) current shell
    (d) none

51. What are >> , << operators?
    (a) append and here document
    (b) appending, reading from multiple files
    (c) reading from multiple files and appending
    (d) none

52. **Sticky bit** setting for a file is for
    (a) protection
    (b) loading into RAM once   and not to unload
    (c) archiving
    (d) none

53. **Sticky bit** for a file can be set by
    (a) owner
    (b) super user
    (c) any of group member
    (d) none

54. **Sticky bit** can be set to
    (a) regular file
    (b) shell script
    (c) binary executable file
    (d) binary file

55. Out of the following two shell scripts which is preferable
     1. **chmod +x $***
     2. **for x in $***
        do
          chmod +x $x
        done
     (a)   both equally   (b)   first one
     (c)   second one   (d)   no comment

56. **SCCS** means
     (a)   source code control system.
     (b)   semi computer controlled system.
     (c)   small computer control system process.
     (d)   none

57. **UNIX Kernel's** task is
     (a)   allocation of CPU to competing process.
     (b)   extending services to system calls.
     (c)   both a & b.
     (d)   only (a).

58. **Process interacts with Kernel**
     (a)   directly by making a system call.
     (b)   indirectly, by being allowed to run.
     (c)   both
     (d)   not applicable.

59. What is not available for a process by default (in terms of file descriptors)
     (a)   0   (b)   1   (c)   2   (d)   3

60. What is the **content of abc** file after the execution of following command   **cp. abc**
     (a)   all files content of P.W.D   (b)   all filenames of P.W.D.
     (c)   command will not run   (d)   none

61. Which of the following is a **popular terminal emulation SW**.
     (a)   perl   (b)   vterm
     (c)   vt100   (d)   smart95

62. What is the effect of the following command executed by root **cp abc /dev/tty1.**
     (a)   error as /dev/tty1 is a device.
     (b)   it will create a file tty1/ in /dev as copy of abc.
     (c)   abc matter appear on terminal tty1 (permissions are assumed to be available)
     (d)   GOK (God only knows!!).

63. **echo $?**
     (a)   no of command line arguments.
     (b)   PID of current shell.
     (c)   integer number indicating exit status of previous command.
     (d)   none

64. If a file **i-node** can support only 10 direct addresses, then what is the maximum file size the file system can handle with them if disk block is 1K.
    (a)   10K   (b)   20K
    (c)   5K   (d)   none

65. What is **maximum file size** that can be addressable using only **single indirection** of 1K blocks with 4 byte block addresses.
    (a)   256 KB   (b)   266 KB
    (c)   16 GB   (d)   none

66. **Swapping** and **paging systems**
    (a)   are same
    (b)   differ in how processes are swapped as a whole or part.
    (c)   not related at all.
    (d)   none

67. Number of **file descriptors** (streams) assigned to any program by default are.
    (a)   2   (b)   3   (c)   7   (d)   none

68. **UNIX kernel's** process table entry is
    (a)   always same as zero.   (b)   same as int.
    (c)   changes in one session.   (d)   is not available at all.

69. The **super block of a bootable partition** consists.
    (a)   Kernel.   (b)   **i-node** list size(no of disk blocks).
    (c)   free blocks list   (d)   1 & 2.
    (e)   b & c.

70. **PATH** environment variable value is useful
    (a)   while shell tries to locate executable of a command.
    (b)   while shell tries to open any file.
    (c)   while shell tries to open any manual page.
    (d)   none

71. What happens if shell locates a program file of a command in a directory which is not having **execution permissions**.
    (a)   message not found appears
    (b)   search continues to next directory.
    (c)   message not found appears if the directory is last in PATH.
    (d)   b & c

72. **wait,** command which suspends operation of terminal till the completion of a background process is _______
    (a)   system call.   (b)   built-in shell command.
    (c)   both   (d)   none

73.   What is the difference between the following commands.
       1. grep From mbox
       2. grep '^From' mbox
       (a)   both are same
       (b)   second command outputs only those lines which starts with word From.
       (c)   **first command outputs** those lines which starts with word From
       (d)   none.

74.   **ls -l | grep '^d'**
       (a)   lists filenames without d character in their name
       (b)   lists sub directory names.
       (c)   both
       (d)   none

75.   In which shell, value of shell variable will become **Hello. How do you do** if you
       initialise with variable(Hello. How do you do).
       (a)   sh   (b)   bourne
       (c)   C Shell   (d)   none

76.   While sending a message through write, which key to be used to execute any shell
       command?.
       (a)   \'   (b)   ?
       (c)   !   (d)   none

77.   What is the output of **A=Test; echo '$A'**
       (a) $A   (b)   A
       (c)   Test   (d)   none

78.   What is the output of **A=ls; echo "$A"**
       (a)   A   (b) $A
       (c)   list of files   (d)   ls

79.   Which program can be used to **change Multiuser** to single user and   vice versa.
       (a)   multiuser   (b)   suser
       (c)   init   (d)   none

80.   **Which level init** program will work in Multiuser mode.
       (a)   S   (b)   2
       (c)   6   (d)   none

81.   **Inittab** file is used to ____.
       (a)   Shut down UNIX machine   (b)   To connect a new terminal
       (c)   To disconnect a modem connection (d)   b & c

82.   If **A=SAR,** echo ________ produces the output SARADA
       (a) $AADA   (b)   `$A`ADA
       (c) ${A}ADA   (d)   none

83. What is the output in found1 and found2
grep root /etc/passwd > found1 2> found2
   (a)   root user information and none   (b)   none and can't open   file
   (c)   root user information and error   (d)   none of the above message

84. When you **login**
   (a)   only.profile executes
   (b)   only /etc/profile executes.
   (c)   profile /etc/profile executes one after another.
   (d)   /etc/profile,.profile executes one after another.

85. Which commands resembles **'more'** command more
   (a)   ed   (b)   pg
   (c)   vi   (d)   cat

86. Which option is used to specify fields separator with **cut** command
   (a)   -f   (b)   -F
   (c)   -d   (d)   none

87. **Cu** command is for ____________
   (a)   control CPU   (b)   to log on a remote system
   (c)   to display file system status.   (d)   none

88. **Cu** resembles
   (a)   cut   (b)   telnet
   (c)   rlogin   (d)   b & c

89. **Take** is used with
   (a)   du   (b)   ftp
   (c)   cu   (d)   none

90. **DEAD** is
   (a)   command   (b)   file
   (c)   environment variable   (d)   none

91. Which **signal can not be trapped.**
   (a)   SIGHUP   (b)   SIGILL
   (c)   SIGKILL   (d)   none

92. **Pipe system call** returns ________ file descriptors.
   (a)   1   (b)   2
   (c)   3   (d)   none

93. **FIFO** can be created using ________ command.
   (a)   makefifo   (b)   mknod
   (c)   both   (d)   none

94. **Korn shell** is compatible mostly with______
   (a)   bash   (b)   csh
   (c)   both   (d)   none

95. What is the output of the following command sequence
   t=How; echo '$t are yo`
   (a) How are you   (b) how
   (c) $t are you   (d) none

96. **Korn shell** does not support.
   (a) arrays   (b) aliasing
   (c) history   (d) none

97. UNIX is written _______ language.
   (a) B   (b) C
   (c) ada   (d) perl

98. **echo **** command output is
   (a) **   (b) file names two times displayed
   (c) once filenames will be displayed   (d) none

99. **Vterm** and **xtalk** are
   (a) terminal emulation SW   (b) terminals
   (c) network SW   (d) none

100. today=Saturday
   What would **echo`today`** and **"today"** will display.
   (a) same   (b) today
   (c) saturday   (d) a & b   (e) none

101. **Multiuser system** should be **necessarily multitasking**
   (a) yes   (b) no
   (c) dubious   (d) none

102. **mv f1 f2 /tmp**
   (a) error
   (b) moves files f1 and f2 to /tmp directory
   (c) f1 will be moved to f2 then f2
   (d) none will be moved to /tmp directory

103. **/bin/passwd**
   (a) contains all users passwords   (b) allows to change password
   (c) same as /etc/passwd file   (d) none

104. **du** displays usage in ______ of P.W.D and it's sub directories.
   (a) MB   (b) blocks
   (c) chains   (d) none

105. **ulimit** command effect will be effective till
   (a) logout by users   (b) permanent if done by the root
   (c) both   (d) none

106. **cron** is
   (a) system command   (b) user command
   (c) daemon   (d) none

107. **Execution** of function ______ than a respective shell script.
    (a) faster
    (b) slower
    (c) easier
    (d) none

108. Which of the following is not **related to at** command.
    (a) atq
    (b) atrm
    (c) hosts.allowed
    (d) at.denied

109. Which are the **UNIX file systems**
    (a) minix
    (b) ext2
    (c) xiafs
    (d) all

110. Which are not related to **news readers**
    (a) pine
    (b) tin
    (c) boon
    (d) inn

111. **"motd"** file is used to display
    (a) motors for sale today
    (b) list of mounted devices
    (c) message today by super user
    (d) none

112. Which of the file gets **executed first**.
    (a) profile
    (b) motd
    (c) login
    (d) news

113. What is the default value of MAILCHECK environment variable.
    (a) /user/spool/mail/
    (b) /user/home
    (c) 600
    (d) none

114. **Tape** is ___ file
    (a) block
    (b) character
    (c) pipe special
    (d) none

115. Which **are not compress commands**
    (a) pack
    (b) compress
    (c) gzip
    (d) tar

116. `who -t` command displays
    (a) displays user names who are for test.
    (b) displays user names whose time quota is exceeded.
    (c) displays user names along with + and - indicating weather they have released messages or not.
    (d) none

117. An **instance of an executing program** known as
    (a) program
    (b) process
    (c) semaphore
    (d) none

118. If **allocated time slice is over**, process will return to ______ state.
    (a) hold
    (b) run
    (c) ready
    (d) none

119. When a process will be **in wait state**?
     (a) queue is full   (b) I/O
     (c) if its time slice is over   (d) none

120. **System accounts** usually need to have user ID's as ___
     (a) 400   (b) 200
     (c) 100   (d) none

121. Any account with UID of O is a _________
     (a) root   (b) super user
     (c) operator   (d) none

122. While **executing a shell script,   shell acts** like
     (a) interpreter   (b) compiler
     (c) OS   (d) none

123. **Shift** command
     (a) backs no arguments   (b) can take one argument (integer)
     (c) b & a   (d) none

124. **ls -l > abc**
     (a) first ls command will be executed.
     (b) first abc file will be created if it is not existing, else it's contents will be wiped
          out.
     (c) b) followed by a) will be carried out by the shell.
     (d) none

125. If you execute **cat <abc >abc** commands on existing abc file what will be the
     contents of abc after execution?
     (a) no change   (b) null
     (c) error   (d) none

126. **cat -u >filename** command
     (a) stores text what you typed till last line if power goes
     (b) unbuffered output
     (c) a & b
     (d) if power goes nothing will be seen in file

127. **ls** command
     (a) is a filter
     (b) is not a filter.
     (c) ls can only be the first command in a pipeline.
     (d) b & probably c

128. You are sending **message** (through write) to a user who has enabled message and
     your terminal is not enabled, What message will you get.
     (a) sorry   (b) connection disconnected
     (c) no reply possible   (d) want to continue

129. In a DOS floppy a file 'Ram' is existing in A:\raj\rani directory,   if one mounts the file in /mnt directory which of the following commands are meaningful.
    (a)   type A:\raj\rani\Ram   (b)   cat /mnt/raj/rani/Ram
    (c)   cat /mnt/A:\raj\rani\Ram   (d)   none

130. If **fsck** finds a file not linked to any directory then it puts in the directory.
    (a)   tmp   (b)   recover
    (c)   lost+found   (d)   none

131. What is the **length of encrypted password**
    (a)   10   (b)   13
    (c)   20   (d)   none

132. Which signal number can not be trapped
    (a)   1   (b)   2
    (c)   9   (d   3

133. **stty -echo**
    (a)   What ever you type appears on screen.
    (b)   What ever you type will not appear on screen.
    (c)   Displays present options of stty.
    (d)   none

134. Is chdir is a
    (a)   shell command   (b)   internal command
    (c)   system call   (d)   none

135. **fork** returns
    (a)   0   (b)   pid of child process
    (c)   both a & b   (d)   none

136. How to make a shell script (ABC) to be **executed in current shell.**
    (a)   ABC   (b)   ABC .
    (c)   . ABC   (d)   none

137. **set** command alone displays
    (a)   environment variables defined   (b)   functions
    (c)   a & b   (d)   none

138. **Functions** in shell script are active in
    (a)   current shell   (b)   sub shell
    (c)   shell in which they are executed   (d)   none

139. If **functions** are executed in a shell
    (a)   new environment will be active even after function completes.
    (b)   new environment will die after function completed.
    (c)   variable values are reset.
    (d)   none

140. `chmod u-s filename` command is
    (a)   not acceptable   (b)   sets set-used-id bit
    (c)   sets sticky bit   (d)   none

141. **Find out** odd-man out of the following
     (a) LINUX   (b) SCO
     (c) NET BSD   (d) XENIX

142. What is the **UID of super user** root ?
     (a) 1   (b) 0
     (c) 100   (d) none

143. Which of the command can be used to create **FIFO file**
     (a) cat   (b) ed
     (c) mknod   (d) vi

144. Which of the following **commands are different**.
     (a) cat   (b) ed
     (c) mknod   (d) vi

145. **Find** the odd man out of the following.
     (a) echo *   (b) ls
     (c) du   (d) none

146. **Find** the odd man out of the following.
     (a) echo '**'   (b) echo **
     (c) echo "**"   (d) none

147. **Find** the odd man out of the following.
     (a) echo x'*'y   (b) echo x*y
     (c) echo x[a-bA-Z0-9]z   (d) x?y

148. **Find** the odd man out of the following.
     (a) ls .*   (b) echo .*
     (c) for x in.; do; echo $x; done; (d) none

149. In standard UNIX system **i-node** information occupies 64 bytes, disk block size is
     512 bytes then in which disk block **i-node** number 32 will be found? Assume block
     addresses are 4 bytes.
     (a) 32   (b) 10
     (c) 5   (d) none

150. If in a disk block 16 **i-node**s can be accommodated then in 6th **i-node** block which
     i-nodes are stored?
     (a) 6-7   (b) 81-96
     (c) none   (d) a &b

151. To access **350008th byte** of a file on 1K block file system,   What level indirect
     block is used. Assume block addresses are 4 bytes.
     (a) single   (b) double
     (c) triple   (d) none

152. **How many disk accesses** are required to fetch information from a disk block which
     can be accessed by triple indirect block ?
     (a) 5   (b) 3
     (c) 2   (d) 7

153. To access byte **350000** of a file how many disk blocks has to be fetched to RAM including **i-node** block and data block?
    (a) 4   (b) 3
    (c) 2   (d) 7

154. Out of the following shell script which will **assign WIN** value to defined variable (x) and exit from the sub-shell
    (a) ${x = WIN   (b) ${x-WIN}
    (c) ${x + WIN}   (d) b & c

155. **Find** Odd man out of the following?
    (a) usenet   (b) telnet
    (c) rlogin   (d) su

156. Which is **odd-man** out of the following.
    (a) usenet   (b) email
    (c) chat   (d) mosaic

157. For **/dev/tty01** and **/dev/tty02** which of the following same?.
    (a) major number   (b) minor number
    (c) both   (d) none

158. **ls -l device file** displays in place of normal size_____ of dev file.
    (a) major   (b) minor
    (c) both   (d) none

159. Identify **odd-man** out of the following.
    (a) terminals   (b) printers
    (c) modems   (d) tape

160. Which is **odd-man** out of the following.
    (a) cat   (b) ed
    (c) vi   (d) emacs

161. **-d** option is used with
    (a) ls   (b) ps
    (c) cpio   (d) both a & c

162. A **process** can explicitly ask for services from the kernel through
    (a) library call   (b) system call
    (c) signals   (d) interrupts

163. The command which **lists all the user ID's** of the system is
    (a) who | cut -d"``-f1   (b) who | wc -l
    (c) cut -d: -f3 /etc/passwd   (d) cut -d: f1 /etc/users

164. The command which gives the **number of users** who are currently logged in the system is
    (a) who | cut -d"``-f1   (b) who | wc -l
    (c) cut -d: -f3 /etc/passwd   (d) cut -d: -f1/etc/users

165. The file which is **executed by the C shell** when the user logs in is
    (a) profile   (b) envsetup
    (c) startup   (d) . login

166. On executing the following commands:
      test=haha
      echo test
      ksh
      echo $test
      (a)   first echo will display "haha" and second will display "test"
      (b)   first echo will display "test" and second will display "haha"
      (c)   first echo will display "test" and second will display nothing
      (d)   first echo will display "haha" and second will display nothing

167. **comm -12 file2 file3 | comm -23 - file1** does the following:
      (a)   prints lines unique to file1, file2 and file3.
      (b)   prints lines unique to file2 and file3 but not present in file1.
      (c)   prints lines present in both file1 and file2, but not present in file3.
      (d)   prints lines present in both file2 and file3, but not present in file1.

168. **uniq -u file1** does the following:
      (a)   prints lines which are repeated in file1.
      (b)   prints lines which are not repeated in file1.
      (c)   prints lines are repeated indicating the number of times they are repeated.
      (d)   prints all lines which are unique in file1

169. **Virtual to physical address translation** is done by the
      (a)   compiler   (b)   loader
      (c)   kernel   (d)   shell

170. **ls -l | tee ls.save | wc**
      In this command the input to wc command is:
      (a)   output of tee command.   (b)   output of ls -l command.
      (c)   the file ls.save   (d)   none of the above

171. Output of the command **echo `who | wc –l`**
      (a)   number of users currently logged in
      (b)   who
      (c)   1
      (d)   none of the above

172. **finger** is a
      (a)   system call   (b)   external command
      (c)   daemon   (d)   none

173. `getopts yn choice` statement a shell script instructs.
      (a)   assigns string yn to variable choice.
      (b)   reads data to variable yn and choice.
      (c)   In command line if you enter -y or -n, choice variable value_become y or n;
             else it becomes? or b.
      (d)   none

174. What is the default value of **OPTIND.**
     (a) 2   (b) 3
     (c) 1   (d) none

175. **What** is the output of
     x=700

     p=x
     eval $p=100
     echo $x
     (a) 700   (b) p
     (c) 100   (d) none

176. **How many bits** are used in UNIX file rights
     (a) 8   (b) 27
     (c) 9   (d) none

177. `chmod 4755 filename` command gives **file permissions as.**
     (a) rwxr-xr-x   (b) rw-rw-rw
     (c) rwsr-xr-x   (d) none

178. **Korn shell** uses information in a ______ environment variable when ever a sub-shell
     is created.
     (a) PROFILE   (b) HOME
     (c) ENV   (d) ENVIRONMENT

179. When **sub shell (Bourne) is created in** Bourne shell.
     (a) profile information is used
     (b) profile information is not used
     (c) either a or b settable by super user
     (d) none

180. **Repeat 3 cat abc | lpr** result is
     (a) displays abc file 3 times   (b) prints 3 copies of abc file
     (c) same as lpr -#3 abc   (d) none

181. The following can look efficiently for thousands of words in parallel.
     (a) grep   (b) egrep
     (c) fgrep   (d) none

182. **"sort + of + o -u filename"** if you run this command on file with words then
     (a) displays all words
     (b) displays all words in the file alphabetical order (only once)
     (c) displays all words sorted according to their sizes
     (d) display unique words.

183. Out of the following, which command that **searches** for all words which contains
     vowels in order.
     (a) grep *ie* filename   (b) grep `*i*e` filename.
     (c) grep "*i*e*" filename   (d) grep *i*e* filename
     (e) b, c & d.

184. What is the out put of **v=can; echo $vnot**
   (a) null						(b) cannot
   (c) error						(d) none

185. **kill -9 $?**
   (a)   background process will be killed
   (b)   system shutdown
   (c)   you will be logged out
   (d)   none

186. What is the output of **who am i | awk '{ print $1}'**
   (a) tty name					(b) time
   (c) user name					(d) none

187. What is the out put of **du -a | awk '{ print $2 }`**
   (a) disk usage					(b) hard disk information
   (c) result similar to ls				(d) none

188. Output of **grep "^From" $MAIL | grep -v marry**
   (a)   all lines containing in file MAIL
   (b)   is same as output of grep '^From' $MAIL|grep -v marry
   (c)   not same as output of
   (d)   list of emails which did not arrive from mary

189. If you open an existing file with **creat system call**
   (a)   previous content will be discarded
   (b)   previous permission will be detained
   (c)   a & b
   (d)   none

190. **No of I/O channels UNIX** can open
   (a) 18						(b) 15
   (c) 20						(d) not fixed

191. **find** command is used to serrate for a file based on ?
   (a) name						(b) owner
   (c) size & time stamps				(d) all

192. Free SW indicates
   (a)   No cost
   (b)   Freely one can sell
   (c)   Liberty to use, modify, and distribute.
   (d)   none

193. Find odd man out of the following (in terms of proprietary aspects)
   (a) SCO UNIX					(b) Windows NT
   (c) Soloris					(d) Linux

194. Find Odd man out of the following.
   (a) Oracle					(b) MySql
   (c) SQL Server					(d) DB2

195. Find the correct one about UNIX/Linux
     (a) Case sensitive OS   (b) Single directory tree
     (c) Secure   (d) All
196. Which of the following are scripting?
     (a) C   (b) C++
     (c) Perl   (d) C#
197. Find odd man out
     (a) UFS   (b) FAT
     (c) NTFS   (d) Win FS
198. Which of the following is earliest development?
     (a) Windows 2.0   (b) X windows
     (c) Mac Windows   (d) Windows XP
199. Find odd man out
     (a) C   (b) C++
     (c) Java   (d) C#
200. Examples of **command languages** are
     (a) C   (b) C shell
     (c) JCL   (d) both b & c
201. How many **links** generally for a directory exists.
     (a) 2   (b) 4
     (c) none   (d) 1
202. When output of a **ls -l** command on a file displays m in the first column then the file is
     (a) machine language file   (b) memory shared file
     (c) created with more command   (d) none
203. File **permissions** can be changed by
     (a) its owner   (b) super user
     (c) both   (d) any of group members
204. System wide **default permissions for a directory** are
     (a) 714   (b) 777
     (c) 644   (d) none
205. Unless you have ___ **permissions to a directory,** you can not enter into it.
     (a) read   (b) execute
     (c) write   (d) none
206. What should be the **umask** value to have 424 as default file   permissions?.
     (a) 0242   (b) 666
     (c) 777   (d) none
207. What should be the **umask** value to have 535 as default directory permissions?
     (a) 761   (b) 0242
     (c) 0222   (d) none

208. Which of the **following commands work** while compiling a.c which calls some mathematical functions?
     1. cc -o a a.c -lm
     2. cc -lm -o a a.c
     (a)   1   (b)   2
     (c)   either   (d)   none

209. **'umask 242'** command makes default file & directory permissions.
     (a)   424, 535   (b)   644, 755
     (c)   424, 555   (d)   none

210. **"chmod u+t dirname"** makes
     (a)   high level protection from
     (b)   any one can test intruders changing, deleting programs
     (c)   not available
     (d)   none

211. **Sticky bit** setting for a directory is for
     (a)   protection   (b)   loading into RAM
     (c)   archiving   (d)   none

212. In **4.1 BSD** Disk block size is
     (a)   2K   (b)   1K
     (c)   512 bytes   (d)   none

213. **Increase in disk block** size ______ file reading times.
     (a)   reduces   (b)   increases
     (c)   not related   (d)   none

214. If **many small files are expected to be stored**, disk block size should be ________.
     (a)   small   (b)   high
     (c)   GOK   (d)   none

215. In a **non-bootable partition** containing files
     (a)   will not have boot block
     (b)   will have boot block with bootstrap loads
     (c)   will have empty boot block
     (d)   none

216. **Super block** contains ________
     (a)   it's size
     (b)   how many maximum files   it can accommodate.
     (c)   a & b
     (d)   b

217. **I-node** table will be
     (a)   on disk   (b)   in memory
     (c)   a & b while system running   (d)   none

218. How often in a typical UNIX, i-nodes table in RAM will be **flushed to Hard Disk.**
     (a)   10 seconds   (b)   20 seconds
     (c)   30 seconds   (d)   it will not happen

219. Which command can update **i-node** table in file system.
     (a)   fsck   (b)   sync
     (c)   fdisk   (d)   none

220. User can ________ **maximum file size** by running ulimit.
     (a)   reduce   (b)   increase
     (c)   a & b   (d)   none

221. If **erase character is set to 'l'** then how can we execute cal command.
     (a)   cal   (b)   we can not execute
     (c)   ca\l   (d)   none

222. How to restore **write** permissions to others to your terminal.
     (a)   mesg   (b)   mesg y
     (c)   changing device permissions   (d)   b & c

223. **trap "ls" 2** in a shell script indicates.
     (a)   ls command gets trapped.
     (b)   when ls gets hanged exit value becomes 2.
     (c)   when you press $\wedge$ C, ls command will be executed on P.W.D.
     (d)   none

224. If an **exported variable is changed in sub-shell** its modified value will be _____ to
     sub-sub-shell.
     (a)   available automatically   (b)   available after exporting again
     (c)   not available at any cost   (d)   none

225. What should be the **umask value** if rwx permissions for user, rx for
     group and none for others?.
     (a)   750   (b)   027
     (c)   022   (d)   none

226. What will be the **i-node** number of root directory?
     (a)   0   (b)   1
     (c)   2   (d)   none

227. What permissions should be given **normal device files** other than   terminal
     (a)   640   (b)   600
     (c)   a & b   (d)   none

228. Which of the following are commonly **world writable?**
     (a)   /tmp   (b)   terminal files /dev
     (c)   /dev/null   (d)   all

229. **rehash** command is found in
     (a)   C shell   (b)   bash
     (c)   korn   (d)   all

230. **ulimit is** ____
    (a)   shell built-in command   (b)   external command
    (c)   system call   (d)   none

231. System **internal name** for a file is
    (a)   filename   (b)   i-number
    (c)   alias   (d)   none

232. **mv file1 file2** (file1 & file2 are specified along with their path) then
    (a)   i-number of file2 will be same as file1.
    (b)   directory entry of i-number will change.
    (c)   directory entry of file1 will disappear.
    (d)   all

233. Which of the following is **dissimilar**.
    (a)   cd   (b)   ls
    (c)   echo   (d)   none

234. What is the **out put of the following command** sequence
    X=$PATH; PATH=; ls; PATH=$X; ls
    (a)   first ls will not be executed
    (b)   listing of P.W.D because of record ls command
    (c)   a & b
    (d)   none

235. A shell script file **abc** can be executed.
    (a)   . abc   (b)   chmod u+x abc; abc
    (c)   sh abc   (d)   all

236. If **umask is set to 777** then **what permissions** you will get for a newly created directory?
    (a)   d---------   (b)   drwxrwxrwx
    (c)   d--x--x--x   (d)   none

237. If you **set umask value as 022** to change default file permissions then what permissions a newly created directory will have ?
    (a)   000   (b)   777
    (c)   755   (d)   none

238. **Default nice value**
    (a)   20   (b)   39
    (c)   0   (d)   none

239. If a process (pid = 177) creates many sub processes then **kill 177** command.
    (a)   kills process 177
    (b)   kills process 177 and all of its children.
    (c)   suspends all child process.
    (d)   none

240. **login** process can be killed by
    (a)   kill followed by its process id   (b)   kill -15 followed by its process id.
    (c)   kill -9 followed by its process id   (d)   none

241. How **many phases** fsck executes
    (a)   2   (b)   5   (c)   7   (d)   none

242. **lost+found** directory will
    (a)   not be in UNIX
    (b)   be under root directory of any partition
    (c)   a & b
    (d)   none

243. **Free i-node** list is in?
    (a)   SUPER block   (b)   boot block
    (c)   **i-node** block   (d)   none

244. **Free data block-list** is seen in
    (a)   boot area   (b)   data area
    (c)   super block   (d)   **i-node** block

245. **size** command is used to find
    (a)   the executable code
    (b)   the initialized portion of the program such as arrays,   string constants, etc.,.
    (c)   the un-initialized data areas
    (d)   all

246. If a program is **compiled with -p** option then the size command on executable file displays size --- than normal.
    (a)   higher   (b)   lower
    (c)   no different   (d)   none

247. With c compiler **which option is used for optimization**?.
    (a)   -c   (b)   -o
    (c)   -O   (d)   none

248. **find / -name "*.bak" -o -name "*.wri" -print ?.**
    (a)   displays files with extension.bak which are under /
    (b)   displays files with extension.wri which are under /
    (c)   both a & b
    (d)   none

249. **ok** is used with _____ command.
    (a)   backup   (b)   find
    (c)   tar   (d)   none

250. **newer** option is used with
    (a)   find   (b)   touch
    (c)   cp   (d)   none

251. **cpio** is
     (a) a command   (b) an option with find
     (c) both   (d) none

252. **ls [-ab]*** displays file names which starts with
     (a) a   (b) b
     (c) a & b   (d) a & b and hypen -.

253. Which one of the following is **not a valid shell** in UNIX.
     (a) csh   (b) jsh
     (c) ksh   (d) msh
     (e) none

254. Which command is used for **changing the permissions**?.
     (a) chper   (b) change
     (c) chmod   (d) give

255. **To know in which shell** we are working in we can use echo
     (a) $SHELL   (b) $Shell
     (c) $shell   (d) $LIST

256. Which of the following command is **not used for communicating with other users?**
     (a) mesg   (b) talk
     (c) write   (c) uucp

257. What will be the command **PS1='binary'** do?
     (a) change the password
     (b) change the prompt
     (c) change the public settings
     (d) change the path to binary   directory

258. **File system checking** is done using:
     (a) fsck   (b) fcks
     (c) sfck   (d) ckfs

259. **Archive** can be taken using the command:
     (a) atr   (b) ar
     (c) tar   (d) none of these

260. **UNIX supports :**
     (a) multi-tasking   (b) multi-user
     (c) a & b   (d) none of these

261. The **utility** to produce **newer versions** along with maintaining the previous
     versions is:
     (a) BCCS   (b) RISC
     (c) SCCS   (d) none of these

262. **Super user** has the **default prompt**:
     (a) $ (b) #
     (c) %   (d) none of these

263. **comm -12 f1 f2** does the following
     (a) prints files in f1 only
     (b) prints lines both in f1 f2
     (c) prints lines in f2 only
     (d) prints lines not common in f1 f2

264. **Command** which deals with raw data and used for data conversion is
     (a) dd
     (b) tar
     (c) cpio
     (d) cat
     (e) none of above

265. If we want to give all **permissions** to owner, read and execute permissions to group of the owner, only execute perm to others, then the command is
     (a) chmod 175 f1
     (b) chmod 751 f1
     (c) chmod 157 f1
     (d) none of the above

266. **tail + 3 f1** will
     (a) starts printing with 3rd line
     (b) starts printing with 4th line
     (c) prints last 3 lines
     (d) none of the above

267. **p1|p2** will
     (a) append standard output of p1 to p2
     (b) connect standard output of p2 to p1
     (c) connect standard output of p1 to p2
     (d) none of the above

268. **The program** which takes user input, interprets it and takes necessary action is
     (a) kernel
     (b) sh
     (c) vi
     (d) scheduler
     (e) none of above

269. **$#** in shell represents
     (a) name of 1st string on command line
     (b) number of command line arguments
     (c) 1st argument
     (d) user has switched to super user
     (e) none of above

270. **To append f1 and f2 to end of a file tmp,** command is
     (a) cat f1 f2 >tmp
     (b) cat f1 f2>>tmp
     (c) cat f2 f1>tmp
     (d) echo f1 f2>>tmp

271. The **excessive movement of pages** back and forth between memory and disk drive due to less memory is called
     (a) swapping
     (b) page fault
     (c) thrashing
     (d) none of above

272. The **default shell** in UNIX OS is
     (a) bourne shell
     (b) csh
     (c) ksh
     (d) jsh

273. **Operating system** hides the details of
     (a) software from the program
     (b) hardware from the user
     (c) functions from the program
     (d) none of the above

274. In the UNIX, each particular program undertaken in the **system** is called
   (a) job   (b) task
   (c) process   (d) none of the above

275. To count the **number of users logged in**, we may give
   (a) who | wc -1   (b) ls | wc -1
   (c) who | wc   (d) none of the above

276. **grep -s Mahatma** file1
   (a) will print lines containing Mahatma in file1
   (b) will print lines not containing Mahatma in file1
   (c) will print the number of times Mahatma appeared in file1
   (d) none of the above

277. **Multiple blank spaces will be replaced by** single blank space in each line of file1
   containing alphanumeric characters
   (a) tr -cs A-Za-z-9'012' " " < file1   (b) tr -c A-Za-z-9'012' " " < file1
   (c) tr -s A-Za-z-9'012' " " < file1   (d) none of the above

278. When you login (C shell) the following **files** are read and executed
   (a) login   (b) profile
   (c) login and.profile   (d) none of the above

279. **ls -l | awk '{ print $2, substr($1, 5, 3)}'**
   (a) prints the filename, its owner and the permission for the group
   (b) number of links, the permission for owner,
   (c) prints the filename, number of links and the permission for group
   (d) none of the above

280. The **function of system administrator does not** include
   (a) repair of damaged file systems   (b) kernel debugging
   (c) disk formatting   (d) none of the above

281. The **subsystem of the kernel** and the hardware which cooperate to translate virtual
   to physical addresses comprises
   (a) the process management subsystem
   (b) the information management subsystem
   (c) the memory management subsystem
   (d) none of the above

282. **UNIX command** is
   (a) part of the program for kernel
   (b) not part of the program for kernel but available as library function
   (c) stand alone program
   (d) none of the above

283. Which of the following **shells** logouts after extended idle period
   (a) sh   (b) csh
   (c) bash   (d) tcsh

284. **r command** is available in
     (a) korn shell   (b) csh
     (c) sh   (d) msh

285. Find **out-odd** man out
     (a) UNIX system V version 4   (b) UNIX system V.4
     (c) B S D 4.4   (d) UNIX S V R 4

286. Find **odd-man** out
     (a) AIX   (b) H P AUX
     (c) NeXt   (d) Linux

287. Find **odd-man** out of the following.
     (a) echo   (b) nobeep
     (c) noglop   (d) shell

288. **file**
     (a) command   (b) environment variable in bash
     (c) built -in shell variable in csh   (d) system

289. **File** name completion is available in
     (a) bourne   (b) bash
     (c) csh   (d) none

290. When a **process** will be halted
     (a) its time slice is exhausted
     (b) it has wait for something to happen
     (c) another process assumed high –priority and CPU is allocated to it.
     (d) all of the above.

291. **User mode** is same as
     (a) unrestricted mode   (b) restricted mode
     (c) kernel mode   (d) none

292. **Responsibilities** of shell are :
     (a) command parsing & file name substitution.
     (b) pipe line hookup.
     (c) environment control & to work as interpretive programming language.
     (d) all

293. Which of the following shells **logouts** after extended idle period.
     (a) sh   (b) csh
     (c) bash   (d) tcsh

294. **cc -o a a.c -I/home/guest/include**
     In the above command **-I option** indicates
     (a) where to look for include files between double quotes in the given C file.
     (b) where to look for include files between angle brackets in the given C file.
     (c) a & b
     (d) none

295. **Shell programming**
     - (a) to be compiled to run
     - (b) can run directly
     - (c) are interpreted language
     - (d) b & c

296. Which of the shells, **foreground process can be moved as background**
     - (a) sh
     - (b) bourn
     - (c) csh
     - (d) none

297. In which shell ~ - **indicates** path of previous working directory ?
     - (a) sh
     - (b) bourn
     - (c) korn
     - (d) none

298. In **which shell** the following is valid statement ?.
     if ["x – y" -ne "x + 2"]
     - (a) sh
     - (b) borne
     - (c) csh
     - (d) Korn

299. Which one of the following **does not accept commands** from a file ?
     - (a) ed
     - (b) sed
     - (c) awk
     - (d) none

300. The implementation of **UNIX by Microsoft** designed to run on microcomputers is
     - (a) linux
     - (b) XENIX
     - (c) POSIX
     - (d) none of the above

301. File name in **UNIX** can be a maximum of
     - (a) 14 characters
     - (b) 11 characters
     - (c) 15 characters
     - (d) none of the above

302. Assume that **try** is a executable program. When we execute **try test.c f** the value of **argc** is
     - (a) 2
     - (b) 4
     - (c) 3
     - (d) none of the above

303. If x=ha then the outcome for **echo $x ha $x** is
     - (a) ha
     - (b) haha
     - (c) hahaha
     - (d) none of the above

304. The shell variable $# gives
     - (a) the number of positional parameters including the command itself
     - (b) the number of positional parameters excluding the command itself
     - (c) exit value of last command
     - (d) none of the above.

305. The **shell startup dot files** for Bourne shell when the user logs on is
     - (a) cshrc
     - (b) .login
     - (c) .profile
     - (d) none of the above

306. If x does not have any value initially then the output of the following execution **echo ${x – 8}** is
     - (a) parameter not set
     - (b) 8
     - (c) x–8
     - (d) x:parameter not found

307. The statement **echo 3 + 4** will display
   (a)   3 + 4   (b)   7
   (c)   blank   (d)   3 4

308. The **shell prompt** can be changed by reassigning the variable
   (a)   PS2   (b)   PS1   (c)   PROMPT   (d)   DISPLAY

309. In **vi to change a word** in command mode one has to type
   (a)   chw   (b)   w   (c)   I   (d)   cw

310. In _______ shell it is possible to **check whether a file** is a   socket or not.
   (a)   sh   (b)   borne   (c)   csh   (d)   korn

311. In which of the following shells it is possible to check whether two files **device and i-node numbers** are same or not using **test** command.
   (a)   sh   (b)   bourne   (c)   csh   (d)   korn

312. Which of the following is **odd-man** out when used within double quotes?.
   (a) $ (b)   ?
   (c)   `(back quote)   (d)   '(single quote)

313. Within which pair of characters backslash characters **does not**   **protects** the character following it from shells evaluation or   expansion?.
   (a)   single quote   (b)   double quote
   (c)   back slash   (d)   back quote

314. In **which shell** the following statements make **primary prompt** string to always display the path of present working directory?.
   (a)   sh   (b)   bourn   (c)   csh   (d)   korn

315. **-F option** meaningful similarly for
   (a)   sed, awk   (b)   awk, grep (c)   sort, awk (d)   none

316. Find out **odd-man** out of the following.
   (a)   bg   (b)   foreach
   (c)   setcnv   (d)   continue

317. In which shell **echo ${xyz[3]}** displays an array element
   (a)   sh   (b)   borne
   (c)   csh   (d)   korn

318. In which shell **echo ${xyz[3]}** displays an array element
   (a)   sh   (b)   borne
   (c)   csh   (d)   korn

319. **int x=1;** statement is valid in ________
   (a)   C language   (b)   bourne shell
   (c)   C shell   (d)   korn shell

320. **default** word is acceptable in ______ shell.
   (a)   sh   (b)   bash   (c)   C   (d)   none

321. Keeping track of resources, to grant resource request, to account for usage and mediating conflicting requests are some of the functions which an **operating system** does as
      (a)   layered extended machine   (b)   resource manager
      (c)   virtual machine   (d)   none

322. Which of the work is **not done by kernel**?
      (a)   handling the transfer of information between computer and terminal
      (b)   keeping track of all programs being run
      (c)   assigning storage for the file
      (d)   none

323. Command " **e filename**" while working with editor causes
      (a)   load the content of filename into ed
      (b)   erasure of the content of the current test buffer and loads the content of default file
      (c)   erasure of the content of the current text buffer and loads content of filename to ed
      (d)   none

324. Command "**ctrl-d**" while working with vi editor cause
      (a)   termination of editing process of the file
      (b)   scrolling the editor window down the test by half a screen full
      (c)   scrolling the editor window up the text by half a screen full
      (d)   none

325. The **grep** command of UNIX is used to
      (a)   sort the records of given file
      (b)   search a file for presence of a string
      (c)   globally replace a string by another
      (d)   none

326. The user **startup file** for Bourne shell is stored in the home directory with name
      (a)   cshrc   (b)   .init   (c)   .startup   (d)   none

327. **All arguments** on command line as individual separate strings are returned by
      (a) $@   (b) $#   (c) $*   (d)   none

328. **Allocation of CPU** to process is done by
      (a)   shell   (b)   scheduler   (c)   getty   (d)   none

329. In **UNIX system facilities** to work together as a team are set by
      (a)   team leader   (b)   system administrator
      (c)   the individual user   (d)   none

330. The **UNIX system calls** are used to
      (a)   inform the system administrator about an abnormal situation
      (b)   obtain some service from the kernel
      (c)   execute a UNIX command from a shell script
      (d)   none

331. Find **odd-man** out of the following
    (a)   X windows   (b)   NeWs
    (c)   open Look   (d)   curses

332. The **kernel** provides
    (a)   process management   (b)   memory management
    (c)   I/O management   (d)   timer management
    (e)   all the above

333. Find **odd-man** out of the following
    (a)   pipes   (b)   named pipes
    (c)   messages   (d)   signal

334. Find **odd-man** out
    (a)   bash   (b)   sh   (c)   csh   (d)   tk

335. **fg** command is not in ______
    (a)   bourn shell (b)   C shell   (c)   korn shell (d)   none

336. Find **odd-man** out of the following
    (a)   C   (b)   C++   (c)   pascal   (d)   perl

337. Find **odd-man** out
    (a)   java   (b)   C   (c)   shell   (d)   perl

338. Find **odd-man** out
    (a)   ed   (b)   ex   (c)   vi   (d)   eq

339. Find **odd-man** out
    (a)   cc   (b)   gcc   (c)   cpp   (d)   as

340. **Permissions file** is available for ______
    (a)   uucp   (b)   tcp   (c)   LLC   (d)   none

341. **/etc/inittab** file fields are separated by ______
    (a)   :   (b)   #   (c)   space   (d)   tab

342. **Ethernet address** is ____
    (a)   36 bits   (b)   48 bits   (c)   24 bits   (d)   none

343. Find **odd-man** out of the following.
    (a)   UDP   (b)   TCP   (c)   port   (d)   IP

344. **UDP** stands for
    (a)   user datagram protocol   (b)   universal data manipulation program
    (c)   user defined path   (d)   none

345. Standard temporary **mount point** is ____
    (a)   /usr   (b)   /var/spool (c)   /home   (d)   /mnt

346. **-nogroup** command is used with

(a)   group   (b)   passwd   (c)   find   (d)   chgrp

347. Find **odd-man** out
      (a)   bash   (b)   rsh   (c)   telnet   (d)   rlogin

348. Find **odd-man** out
      (a)   more   (b)   less   (c)   cat   (d)   ed

349. Find **odd-man** out ________
      (a)   find   (b)   locate   (c)   whereis   (d)   PATH

350. Find **odd-man** out
      (a)   jobs   (b)   at   (c)   batch   (d)   none

351. Find **odd-man** out
      (a)   while   (b)   repeat
      (c)   foreach   (d)   for

352. In UNIX system, at any one time
      (a)   only one process is running
      (b)   several processes generally are running
      (c)   only in computers having multiple processors, more than one process can be
            running
      (d)   none

353. UNIX can have
      (a)   one file system only
      (b)   n file systems, it had n hard disks
      (c)   any number of file systems depending upon space on the disk
      (d)   none

354. Filter is a program which
      (a)   reads input, processes it and writes the output
      (b)   uses either redirection or pipe
      (c)   takes flow of data from standard input, processes it and sends the results on the
            standard output
      (d)   none

355. The user startup file Bourne shell is stored in the home directory with the name
      (a)   .shrc   (b)   .login   (c)   .init   (d)   none

356. In " for I in * ", the value list for variable I is taken from
      (a)   filenames in PWD   (b)   command line arguments
      (c)   environment variables   (d)   none

357. In awk $0 stands for
      (a)   the command   (b)   first field of the record
      (c)   entire record   (d)   none

358. The following is not a UNIX shell
      (a)   C shell   (b)   perl   (c)   korn shell (d)   none

359. The default shell, which is to be used when a user logs in, is defined in
    (a)   /etc/shell file   (b)   /etc/passwd file
    (c)   startup file in the user home directory (d)   none

360. System calls are
    (a)   part of UNIX kernel
    (b)   other name for UNIX commands
    (c)   basically part of library functions in UNIX
    (d)   none

361. The hidden file in UNIX
    (a)   have special status bit associated with the file descriptor
    (b)   have name starting with dot
    (c)   can be accessed only by OS kernel
    (d)   none

362. **NFS** is
    (a)   stateless   (b)   statefull   (c)   both   (d)   none

363. **uucp** is
    (a)   batch processing   (b)   time sharing   (c)   swapping   (d)   none

364. **Resolver's** objective is to reduce load on _____ server
    (a)   name   (b)   file   (c)   ftp   (d)   none

365. **rsh** uses _________ TCP connections.
    (a)   1   (b)   2   (c)   3   (d)   none

366. Who handles **wildcards**?
    (a)   kernel   (b)   shell   (c)   file system (d)   none

367. Irrespective of **login or sub shell** same configuration file (pointed by the environment variable **ENV**) is used in _________ shell
    (a)   bourne   (b)   korn   (c)   C   (d)   none

368. Memory Management Unit (**MMU**) **registers** are accessible in _____ mode.
    (a)   user   (b)   kernel   (c)   both   (d)   none

369. Find odd man out
    (a)   context switch   (b)   mode switch
    (c)   execution context   (d)   none

370. **fork()** system call doesn't
    (a)   reserve swap space for child
    (b)   return PID of the parent to child
    (c)   put child in scheduler queue
    (d)   allocate new PID and process structure to child

371. The **exit()** function doesn't perform _____
    (a)   turns-on all the signals   (b)   closes all open files
    (c)   wakes up parent   (d)   none

372. A **pipe** can have many ______
    (a)   readers   (b)   writers   (c)   both   (d)   none

373. Find odd man out
    (a)   s5fs   (b)   FFS   (c)   FAT   (d)   xiafs

374. Files indirect blocks are in __________ of partition
    (a)   boot area   (b)   super block   (c)   system call   (d)   data area

375. C# equivalent in Linux
    (a)   perl   (b)   ruby   (c)   mono   (d)   python

376. Which is most widely used as Web Server
    (a)   IIServer   (b)   weblogic   (c)   apache   (d)   none

377. Find odd man out
    (a)   perl   (b)   python   (c)   shell scripts   (d)   C Language

378. Where users pass words are stored in UNIX/Linux
    (a)   /etc/passwd   (b)   /etc/shadow   (c)   both   (d)   none

379. What is the PID of init process?
    (a)   1   (b)   0
    (c)   we can not say   (d)   65536

380. Which is odd man out of the following?
    (a)   cut   (b)   grep   (c)   cat   (d)   sort

381. What is not true about cut command?
    (a)   it extracts both words and characters from each line of a file
    (b)   it works similar to SELECT command of SQL
    (c)   it can not change natural order of fields in the output
    (d)   all

382. Which is not an editor?
    (a)   vi   (b)   vim   (c)   cat   (d)   emacs

383. Which is not a archiving utility in Linux/UNIX?
    (a)   tar   (b)   rpm   (c)   zip   (d)   cat

384. The command which has –o option
    (a)   cut   (b)   paste   (c)   sort   (d)   grep

385. Which command in UNIX/Linux can be used similar to SQL
    (a)   cut   (b)   cat   (c)   sort   (d)   awk

386. Shell is
    (a)   system SW   (b)   command line interpreter
    (c)   intelligent parser   (d)   all

387. The shell having better precision is
    (a)   bash   (b)   csh   (c)   korn   (d)   jsh

388. Find odd man out
    (a)   LaTeX   (b)   vi   (c)   vim   (d)   emacs

389. Find odd man out
      (a)   xdvi   (b)   psview   (c)   ghostview   (d)   lpr

390. By default, in which directory users directories are found in UNIX/Linux?
      (a)   /   (b)   /HOME   (c)   /home   (d)   /users

391. Where do we find our mail box?
      (a)   /home   (b)   /usr/home (c)   /var/spool/mail   (d)   /mail

392. The command to chat in UNIX/Linux in command mode is
      (a)   write   (b)   chat   (c)   talk   (d)   none

393. The symbolic link
      (a)   can be created for directory   (b)   can be created for files of other partition
      (c)   both a & b are wrong   (d)   both a & b are true

394. Find incorrect one
      (a)   linux runs only on 8085   (b)   linux runs only 386 and above
      (c)   linux runs on Itanium also   (d)   linux runs on AMD PC also

395. Which OS is commercial one out of the following?
      (a)   Linux   (b)   BSD
      (c)   Soloris   (d)   OS/7 Warp

396. du command displays file size in
      (a)   bytes   (b)   kilo bytes (c)   blocks   (d)   none

397. Which is equivalent command in DOS for Linux command "rm –R".
      (a)   erase   (b)   delete   (c)   deltree   (d)   none

398. Under which License Linux is released
      (a)   World Trade License   (b)   Indian License
      (c)   GPL (GNU Public License)   (d)   linux License

399. Binaries means
      (a)   source files   (b)   libraries
      (c)   device drivers   (d)   executable programs

400. Scheduling used in UNIX/Linux
      (a)   FCFS   (b)   round robin
      (c)   round robin with priorities   (d)   optimal

401. Find odd man out
      (a)   more command is available in Windows also
      (b)   more command of Linux is same as Windows
      (c)   djgpp is free C/C++ compiler for Windows
      (d)   gcov command works under windows

402. Which is not true?
      (a)   Windows XP is also 32 bit OS   (b)   Linux is also 32 bit OS
      (c)   Windows 3.1 is a OS   (d)   none

403. Find odd man out
  (a)   Windows Vista   (b)   Windows Workgroups
  (c)   Windows 98   (d)   Windows XP

404. Which is forth coming OS from Microsoft
  (a)   Windows Vista   (b)   Windows Workgroups
  (c)   Windows 98   (d)   Windows XP

405. DOS means
  (a)   disk operating system   (b)   distributed operating system
  (c)   denial of aervice   (d)   all

406. Find odd man out
  (a)   ftp   (b)   telnet   (c)   arp   (d)   squid

407. Which system call is used to create a process in UNIX/Linux?
  (a)   create_process() (b)   execl() (c)   fork()   (d)   none

408. Which command is used to find whether remote user is currently working or not in
     UNIX/Linux?
  (a)   ckuser   (b)   finger   (c)   arp   (d)   ping

409. To check the connectivity which command is used?
  (a)   ckuser   (b)   finger   (c)   arp   (d)   ping

410. Which of the following is odd one?
  (a)   tail   (b)   head   (c)   cat   (d)   find

411. Which one is odd one?
  (a)   chown   (b)   chmod   (c)   chgrp   (d)   chattr

412. Which is odd one in terms of permissions?
  (a)   Windows NT   (b)   AIX   (c)   Novell   (d)   DOS

413. Defragmentation is not available in
  (a)   Windows 95   (b)   Windows XP (c)   Linux   (d)   none

414. In UNIX/Linux
  (a)   till recently group based security is supported
  (b)   root user itself probable vulnerable place
  (c)   ACL's are supported recently
  (d)   all

415. Kill command can be
  (a)   used by any user to kill any one's process
  (b)   remove any ones file
  (c)   used by a user to kill his process
  (d)   none

416. Which file is used to set environment variables by the system
  (a)   /etc/init   (b)   /etc/inittab (c)   /etc/profile (d)   /etc/configure

417. Find odd man out
  (a)   perl   (b)   python   (c)   Shell Scripts   (d)   **C Language**

418. Exit status of a program in Linux/UNIX
     (a) $$ (b) $. (c) **$?** (d) $!

419. Find odd man out of the following
     (a) text (b) stack (c) data (d) **binary**

420. Optimization option for gcc
     (a) –opt (b) **–O** (c) –o (d) -optimize

421. Header files contains
     (a) function signatures (b) function calls
     (c) function definitions (d) none

422. Arguments of a function are pushed into stack in a C programs execution
     (a) last first (b) first last (c) arrays first (d) pointers first

423. 32 bit computer means
     (a) address bus width is 32 bits (b) it can theoretically access 4GB memory
     (c) data bus width is 32 bits (d) all

424. Option to be used with gcc to debug the code
     (a) –d (b) –g (c) –O (d) -Wall

425. Find odd man out
     (a) PCB (b) swap (c) page table (d) Filename

426. Preprocessor
     (a) cc1 (b) pp (c) cpp (d) as

427. To remove symbol table
     (a) assembler (b) first pass assembler
     (c) rm (d) strip

428. Turbo C generated binary file
     (a) dynamically linked (b) statically linked
     (c) user can specify (d) both will be created

429. Find odd man out
     (a) ELF (b) EXE (c) a.out (d) PIE

430. Find incorrect one
     (a) int main()
     (b) int main(int argc)
     (c) int main(int argc, char **argv, char **y)
     (d) none

431. Ah
     (a) 32 (b) 16 (c) 8 (d) none

432. _____ register value is considered as exit status
     (a) eax (b) ebx (c) ecx (d) edx

433. ____ instruction we have to call for executing a system call in assembly
    (a) int 0 × 17 (b) int 0 × 23 (c) int 0 × 80 (d) none

434. exit()
    (a) 1 (b) 2 (c) 3 (d) 4

435. If we want to execute write() system call in assembly
    (a) 4 has to be moved to eax
    (b) 3 has to be moved to ebx
    (c) file descriptor has to be moved to eax
    (d) none

436. ____ %eax, %eax gives zero in eax
    (a) add (b) sub (c) xorl (d) none

437. A Linux/UNIX File contains
    (a) major number (b) minor number
    (c) both (d) none

438. Bootstrap program loads to
    (a) 07890h (b) 07C00h (c) 08C00h (d) 0 × B800

439. Boot strap program should end with
    (a) AA66h (b) AA55h (c) AAAAh (d) none

440. Daemon
    (a) a set of functions (b) a program
    (c) a program looks at some port (d) none

441. Boorstrap program size in Windows
    (a) 500 bytes (b) 512 bytes (c) 446 bytes (d) 984 bytes

442. Command to automate SW development and reduce compilation time
    (a) strip (b) skip (c) make (d) gdb

Fill in the Blanks

1. **typeset** command is acceptable in ___________ shell.

2. **-q option** in **ls** command produces ___________

3. If there is an **unprintable character in a filename** then **ls** command displays its name with ___________ at the position of unprintable character.

4. **OFMT** is used with ___________ command.

5. **fi** and **endif** are counterparts in ___________ shell and ___________ shell.

6. **elif** equivalent in **C shell** is ___________

7. **breaksw** statements equivalent in **Bourne shell** is ___________

8. The **shell acts** like ___________ interpreter.

9. The **kernel process** will have ___________ priority.

10. The **user passwords** details in UNIX are kept in ___________ file.

11. There are ___________ **standard files** in UNIX.

12. The **file descriptor** for **stdio** in UNIX is ___________

13. The command **to remove a directory** in UNIX is ___________

14. **Two files can be merged together** using the ___________ command at the command line.

15. When **a file is created the default access permissions** are ___________

16. The **default standard error** file is ___________

17. **cat xyz -** will concatenate xyz with the input from the ___________

18. The **output of a command can be directly fed into the input of another command** using a ___________

19. The **user created shell variables** must start with an ___________

20. The shell variable that defines **intermediate field separator** is ___________

21. By changing ___________ environment variable **UNIX prompt** can be changed.

22. ___________ command in Bourne shell can be used to make a shell variable available in sub shell.

23. The **startup instructions** for a users account can be kept in the ___________ file.

24. ___________ is the **shell program name** in a shell script.

25. The **$*** in a shell script stands for all the arguments except the ___________

26. The **exit status** of (after execution) a command is retained in ___________

27. ___________ command can be used to **assign value of an expression** to a variable.

28. ___________ is used to **separate commands** in a line.

29. **Commands can be grouped together** by writing ___________

30. If **command1** is to be executed only if **command2** fails, you write them as ________

31. **ls -a |paste - - - -**   displays ___________

32. ___________ is used to **denote a comment** in a shell script.

33. ___________ denotes a **do nothing** command in shell scripts.

34. The **system call open** returns ___________ if the file can be opened.

35. The **read system call** returns ___________ read.

36. To **split a file** vertically ___________ command can be used.

37. **New process can be created** using the ___________ system call.

38. The **write system call** writes into a file from the ___________

39. **Two hard linked files** share the same ___________

40. **ls -b** lists ___________ characters as octal values in file names.

41. An **unsuccessful command** returns ___________ value as exit code.

42. ___________ can be used **to recover a file** xyz which was aborted while it is been editing previously through vi.

43. ___________ command can be used to **make a printer as a default** printer.

44. A single command which lists all files in a directory, distinguishing between a directory, executable and symbolic link files is ___________

45. When a **file system is mounted on a directory**, the files previously present in that directory ___________ accessible.

46. **delta** is a ___________ related command

47. In korn shell **ls ~** displays ___________

48. In korn shell **"echo ~+"** displays _____________

49. The _____________ process is called the **parent process** all users commands.

50. During **execution of a process, CPU references** the _____________ address of a page.

51. _____________ **function gives the process number** of the present process in a C program.

52. _____________ **command** associates a directory with a device.

53. _____________ allows **interactive dialogue between users** at two different terminals.

54. The **secondary system prompt** is denoted by _____________

55. The **first version of UNIX** was developed by _____________ on DEC PDP series.

56. **Command to see** various processes running on the system is _____________

57. **echo *** will print _____________

58. _____________ **command** allows you to see which users are currently logged in the system.

59. _____________ is the **exit status** of last command.

60. _____________ is **general tool for separating** character strings.

61. _____________ is used to make a command to **execute with lower priority.**

62. _____________ **updates the time of last modification** of a file.

63. _____________ is a tool for **checking grammar.**

64. **awk -F: `{ print $7 }` /etc/passwd |sort| uniq -c** displays _____________

65. **awk -F: `{print $7}' /etc/passwd |sort| uniq -d** displays _____________

66. If a C language program consists a line #include "abc.h" while compiling, preprocessor **checks in the directories** _____________ and _____________

67. **-I option with cc** command informs c compiler _____________

68. **Standard C library name is** _____________ which contains _____________

69. **awk -F: '{print $7 }' /etc/passwd | sort | uniq -u** displays _____________

70. awk -F: '{print $7}' /etc/passwd | sort | uniq -d displays _____________

71. **Context switching** means _____________

72. **mail** and **write** differs in _____________

73. **Extended instructions** of operating system defining interface with operating system and user is known as _____________

74. **Connecting output of a program to the input of another program** without temporary file is done through __________

75. Changes made to __________ variables in **parent shell** are automatically transmitted to child process.

76. **Pattern scanning** and processing __________ language

77. **Execution of system call** is done in __________ mode.

78. __________ **switches the machine** from **user mode** to **kernel mode**.

79. In **UNIX,** __________ is used to locate file internally.

80. **vi** is __________ editor.

81. **sed** is generalization of __________

82. In **Bourne shell,** the local variable is made global by using __________

83. We may know by using __________ **command whether existing file is a directory.**

84. **Condition operator** __________ causes whether existing file is a directory.

85. **User defined arithmetic variables** in awk are initialized to __________ by default.

86. The **concept of region in UNIX** is __________ of the memory management policies implemented by the operating system.

87. In **C program** you may execute **UNIX command x by using function** __________

88. **Encrypted password information** of user is stored in __________

89. To **create poster,** command is __________

90. To **change the prompt string** we have to change __________

91. The **same file which runs** automatically for all users before login __________

92. To give **message to all logged in users** simultaneously ______

93. After **improper shutdown** __________ program is executed during booting.

94. **Name of file** is stored in __________ which file is placed

95. **Free data blocks are arranged** as __________

96. **diff f1 f2** prints __________ file f1.

97. **wc counts** __________ of file.

98. **tail f1** prints __________ of file f1.

99. **who | sort** prints __________ logged in machine.

100. **/etc** directory contains ____________ files.

101. By giving __ in end of command. it is executed in ____________

102. **?** matches ____________ character where as ____________ matches group of any characters in a file.

103. **p1 || p2** means run p2 if ____________

104. **Chmod** ____________ f1. will make file f1 executable by all users.

105. **Core** files will be created when ____________

106. **find /aab -name "*.bak" -print** command displays ____________

107. **find /home -name "*.*" -atime +3 -print** displays ____________

108. **find /home \(-name "*.c" -o -name "*.pas" \) -print** displays ____________

109. **cpio stands for** ____________

110. The following command ____________
     find /home/venkat -newer /home/venkat/log -print| cpio -o>/dev/rmt1

111. **fcntl** system call provides control of operation on the file at file descriptor level, where as ____________ provides device level.

112. **stime** allows ____________ user to set global kernel variable that gives the current time.

113. **chdir()** changes current directory of ____________

114. With **grep** command to find lines containing only a particular **string** in a file (abc) the command is ____________

115. In the command **grep ^[^a-z] abc** first circumflex (^) means lines begins with and second circumflex means ____________

116. ____________ **command to copy variable** to sub shells.

117. ____________ can **change system date**

118. ____________ can be used a message on another user screen.

119. ____________ command to be used **to embed two files** side by side.

120. The heart of UNIX is ____________

121. ____________ is the command to **copy UNIX files to DOS** format.

122. A pipe which is created in a process is ____________ by the child process created through fork() after the pipe is created.

123. ____________ are equivalent to **INTERRUPTS in DOS**.

124. ____________ command is used for **moving files**/directories.

125. _____________ is the command to know the information about **particular user on the net**.

126. The **layer surrounding the kernel** is the _____________

127. A **program in execution** is called a _____________

128. In UNIX filenames can be upto _____________ **characters** long.

129. **UNIX is organized** as a _____________ structure.

130. _____________ is a process that performs a task for the OS on a regular basis.

131. _____________ and **Denis Ritchie wrote the UNIX** kernel for first time in C.

132. _____________ are program that perform **simple transformation** on data (files) as it flows through them.

133. The program _____________ reports the **correspondence between device** files and directories.

134. **Redirecting output** of a command to the file _____________ causes the output to be thrown away.

135. Using the _____________ command one can **create an empty file** without using any edit utilities.

136. The _____________ **utility compares two files line by line.**

137. The _____________ utility makes a **byte by byte comparison.**

138. The **library call** _____________ changes the size of the allocated memory block to a new size.

139. The _____________ command allows the user to **run any command** such that it continues **even after logout.**

140. In **awk** the variables **NR** stands for _____________ .

141. **awk ' $0 ~ /^$/{x=x+1} END { print x}' filename** displays _____________

142. _____________ **awk script** to display listing of directory specified along the command line along with only size and name.

143. **Spool** means _____________

144. **make** command looks for _____________ or _____________ .

145. **mknod** command is used to _____________

146. **Loader** command _____________

147. **strip** command is used to _____________

148. **ld** command is the linking loader which _____________

149. **ls -la | grep `` `^d` `` ** command displays ___________

150. **ls -la | cut -d " " -f 2** display ___________

151. **ls -al | tail +2 | wc -l** displays ___________

152. If file aa is hard linked via a file aaa their **i-node** number are ___________

153. **I-node** number of symbolic link file is ___________ as that of the linked file.

154. If a **foreground job is suspended** by entering and the same can be made background by ___________ command.

155. In executable files, **magic number** size is ___________ long.

156. `` `find / -nouser -print` `` command displays ___________

157. **I-node** table is kernel table data structure which holds ___________ all the **i-node** of currently open files and directories

158. Normally **i-node** 1 is reversed for ___________ handling.

159. For example, block 2 is beginning of **i-node** list and that there are 8 **i-node**s per block, then **i-node** number 33 will be available in disk block number ___________

160. **rehash** is used to ___________ internal table of C shell.

161. After a **system crash**, to recover the file content ___________ option has to be used with vi.

162. ___________ message against **unmount command** indicates device which is to be unmounted is in use.

163. A user ___________ **change his password as his username.**

164. `` `cat /etc/passwd | cut -d: -f1,2 | grep `*` | cut -f1 | sort` `` displays sorted usernames whose password is___________

165. When you **log in,** if the **function has to be loaded automatically** their definitions can be ___________ file.

166. In newer versions of **UNIX (system V),** if you **set stick bit** to a directory _______

167. `` `chmod +t dirname` `` sets ___________

168. Terminal devices will be owned by user when logs in and will be owned by ___________ when he logs out.

169. To display lines of file which ends with any digit using grep can be achieved by ___________

170. **ctrl + Z** in DOS is end of **file marker,** same in UNIX is ___________

171. 0, 1 and 2 are **file descriptors** of ___________, ___________ and ___________ .

172. **File descriptor** is an integer whereas file pointer is a ___________

173. ___________ xyz (xyz executable binary file) makes the xyz once executed it will not be **swapped out of swap** device.

174. ___________ is the **maximum acceptable PID number in UNIX**.

175. **Compiling with optimization flag** set makes program execution ___ and Compilation ___________

176. **UID and GID** of root are ___________ and ___________ respectively.

177. **DES** stands for ___________

178. **ls [!aeiou]*** command lists files ___________

179. **When listed character and block special files**, file size entry in this files indicates ___________

180. When **major and minor device** numbers of a /dev/ttyS0 are 4 and 64 respectively, then major and minor device number of /dev/ttyS1 will be ___________

181. **Block special files** will have ___________ and character special files will have ___________ I/O.

182. If the number of direct block addresses are 12 and disk block size is 4K then the **max file size without use of indirect** addressing is ___________

183. **cmchk** displays ___________ in bytes.

184. **Boot block** contains ___________

185. **df** displays ___________

186. **"copy filename+,, "** is a DOS command to change time stamp of a file. It's equivalent command in UNIX is ___________

187. ___________ command displays **last access time of a file**.

188. **sort** command sorts lines of a file according to ___________ collating sequence.

189. **"-u "** option with sort is for to ___________ and with **touch** command is to know ___________

190. **-c1-5** option with **cut** command displays ___________ line of specified files.

191. **Default separator** which cut command assumes is ___________

192. **uustat** is to ___________

193. ___________ indicates where **partially interrupted** mails can be stored.

194. ___________ system call is used to create message queues during interprocess communication.

195. **vi a1.c; cc -o a !$**
 In the above command sequence meaning of !$ is ___________

196. **touch** command is used to ___________ of files.

197. **File descriptor** and **File pointers** are ___________.

198. **0, 1 and 2** are **file descriptors** of ___________, ___________ & ___________.

199. With **more** command space bar is used to display next screen, Where as ___________ used with **pg** command to do the same.

200. While viewing a file using **pg, $ command** can be used to ___________

201. Output of the two command sequences **v=can; echo ${v}not** is ___________

202. **who|awk '{ print $5, $1 }' |sort** prints ___________

203. When a **system call** incurs an error, it stores the reason in an ___________ variable named ___________

204. The global variable **sys_err** defines ___________ value to errno.

205. **Close system call** will fail if ___________

206. In **C shell, alias** command ___________

207. **alias lstl ls -t|sort; lstl** output is ___________

208. **ls -ld ~** commands output in C shell is ___________

209. Output of **B = command** makes B value ___________

210. **Buffered I/O reduces** ___________, ___________ and improves ___________.

211. **who** program uses file /etc ___________.

212. ___________ **function returns true** if its arguments is either 0-9 or A-F.

213. The **dup system call** ___________.

214. Maximum file size in an UNIX machine which uses 1K disk blocks, **i-nodes** with double indirect blocks is ___________.

215. In **C shell** output of following sequence of commands ___________.
 set job = ("HELLO how" you); shift job; echo $job[1]

216. When will it happen consecutive disk blocks are available, but file can not be created? ___________.

217. In **C shell** which one executes first **.cshrc** or **.login** ? ___________.

218. **env** or **printenv** commands displays ___________.

219. **unset** or **unsetenv** commands are used to ___________.

220. What will be the output for **echo $PS1** command ___________.

221. **savehist** variable ___________.

222. **USER variable** is a variable in ___________ shell.

223. **repeat 4 popd** ___________.

224. **Daemon** is a ___________.

225. **Daemon** process uses ___________ files.

226. **Kernel panic** message indicates ___________.

227. ___________ is a developing standard for an "open" computer operating system that is similar to UNIX.

228. **Boot block** contains ___________.

229. **File descriptor** is small positive integer whereas **file pointer** is ___________

230. ___________ is a table which describes all processes in the system at any point of time.

231. In **C shell echo $?xxx** displays 1 which indicates ___________

232. **>&** in **C shell** is used to ___________.

233. **>>& filename** directive with a command makes shell to append ___________ to the specified filename.

234. Which directive is required in **C shell** to connect standard error also in piping ?

235. **dirs** command in **C shell** displays ___________

236. **globe *** in **C shell** displays ___________

237. **Login** file can be used to ___________ and should be in ___________.

238. **Nohup** with a command is used to ___________

239. If you give you a command as an argument to **nohup** that command will be run with ___________ signals ignored.

240. **repeat 3 echo hello** displays ___________.

241. **set noglob; echo *; unset noglob; echo *; echo ???** displays ___________

242. Only ___________ may **violate many of the file protection** rules of OS (UNIX).

243. A ___________ is a **specialized form of a file** which maintains a list of all files in it.,

244. For duplicating a line in vi, we bring the cursor on the line press ___________

245. In **ed editor,** the command ___________ allows to see the default workfile name.

246. The **scope of shell variable can be made global** to the sub shell by the ___________ command.

247. To **perform actions before reading the first record** of the file in awk we write ___________

248. ___________ means the **program tried to reference an area of memory** that it was not allowed to.

249. If **PATH variable is unset**, then the command search defaults to the directories ___________

250. **New process can be created** using the ___________ system call.

251. **Command providing super user status** is ___________

252. ___________ to **continue running process** even if user logs out.

253. ___________ command is used to do **any pending I/O** operations.

254. **Thrashing** means ___________

255. ___________ command can be used **to remove a print job**.

256. **For loops** equivalent in **C shell** is ___________ .

257. **cdpath** shell variable in C shell controls ___________ command.

258. **cdpath** shell variables (in **C shell**) counterpart in bash is ___________

259. Output of **readonly** command is ___________

260. An **environment** is ___________

261. **set argv = (-a 10 -b 70 -c 81); shift; echo $argv; echo $#argv** the above command displays ___________

262. **pushd** command in C shell is used to ___________

263. **echo $history** displays ___________ remember now.

264. Output of the following command sequence is ___________
     set history = 1; ls; history

265. The output of following sequence of commands is ___________
     set p="/user/bin   /bin /tmp"; echo $p.

266. The equivalent command in Bourne shell for **C shell is** ___________
     set prompt="hello".

267. In **shell script,** first line looks like **#!/bin/**name (name can be sh or bash, csh), it conveys that ___________

268. The following command **rm proj*\mno** ___________

269. In ___________ **process share a portion of memory**; when one process completes writing to this memory, the other process may read the data.

270. **Interrupts** may have priorities, whereas signals ___________ such differentiation.

271. **Inter-process communication** is done through ___________, ___________, ___________, ___________.

272. **Devices are integrated into the file system** and are known as ___________

273. ___________ are **indices** into the process's open file table.

274. ___________ is used to index **an array containing the driver entry pointers**.

275. **pipe call** creates ___________ of a pipe.

276. **XENIX is** ___________ company product

277. **Process creates** by ___________ user are privileged.

278. **sync system** call ___________

279. When a **shell starts another shell**, the ___________ shell is created.

280. A **system process known** as ___________ which checks and sees is there any other process is running on (remote) device.

281. In **/etc/gettydefs** file fields are separated by ___________

282. In some **secure systems** only ___________ and ___________ can access **/etc/shadow** file.

283. **/etc/group** file contains ___________

284. One **UNIX system can call** another and log into the system as ___________ user.

285. **BASH** means ___________

286. In both Korn and C shell ___________ command can be used to **check list of aliases**.

287. **dirs** command is in ___________ shell.

288. If a **command executable file is not find** then you will get ___________ error message.

289. A **command when enclosed** between ___________ the output of that command is passwd to the program as arguments.

290. **wc>!xyz** is valid in ___________ shell.

291. ___________ command can be used **to change your default shell**.

292. If you want to search for a **word** anywhere in the history buffer, you can use ___________ command.

293. ___________ command displays when someone was **last logged into the system**.

294. **perl** ___________

295. In **perl -e** at command line indicates ___________

296. In **perl** ___________ is used to **enclose a string**.

297. In shell single quotes for a variable leave its contents unevaluated; **double quotes** ___________ its contents.

298. In perl the following statements displays ___________
@xyz=('zzz', 'mmm');
print @xyz

299. **Associate array** means ___________

300. **<STDIN>** is ___________

301. **KAP** is ___________ for C.

302. The **executable file header** consists of ___________

303. **/usr/include/a.out.h** file contains ___________

304. **String table in executable file** ___________

305. ___________ command is used **to reduce the size of an executable** file.

306. If there is **no makefile(s) defined**, then make hello.c ___________

307. While **compiling the C program generated by lex**, ___________ option should be given.

308. **Ethernet addresses** are ___________ layer addresses.

309. In 48 bits of Ethernet addresses ___________ **bit designate** vendor?.

310. In **IP address** first (primary) octet value ___________ is used for **loopback** testing.

311. **Port number** for E-mail is ___________

312. **Finger daemon** is set through ___________ file.

313. **XDR** ___________

314. Well defined **port for RPC** is ___________

315. **-x option with ls** command ___________

316. **-nouser** option is used with ___________ command.

317. **find / -size + 2048 –print** command displays ___________

318. **find / -size -2048 –print** command displays ___________

319. **chsh** is used to ___________

320. **smurf** is ___________

321. **man -k** command is same as ___________

322. **rpcgen** ___________

323. Global **"environment" variables** which are used to configure the default behavior of a variety of programs in an ___________ array for each process.

324. The output of `which cd` command is ___________

325. In C shell **which** is a built-in command whereas in Bourne shell it is ___________

326. The following command in some PC OS's will work and the same will not work in UNIX because ___________
      rename *.x *.y

327. The following two commands on a file (a.c) when executed the result is
      ____
      egrep '(^#)'   a.c
      egrep '(^[^#])' a.c

328. Command to **Print all lines NOT beginning with uppercase**

329. Command to **print all lines of a file containing ! * & but not starting with #**

330. **Scripts** should be readable also in addition to executable because ___________

331. To make a file **regardless of who runs the program** ___________

332. ___________ information will be conveyed by the **first 4 bits of a** files mode bits.

333. A **directory for which the sticky bit is set** ___________ of files within it.

334. A file or directory inside a directory with the **t-bit** set can only be deleted or renamed by its ___________.

335. **set** and **unset** commands are available in ___________ shell.

336. **If ($?variable)** expression will be true ___________

337. In C shell to define a environment variable the following style is used
      setenv VAR   "VALUE"
      whereas to define a shell variable
      set VAR ____ "VALUE" is used.

338. What is the **output of the following sequence** of commands when executed interactively.
      set A = ("a b c d")
      echo $A[$#A]

339. By executing ___________ command in C shell **files will not be overwritten** by the
      `>' command.

340. If **ls >>&pqr** executed then it ___________

341. **Wildcards** do not work inside ___________

342. A jobs process id is 333 and it is suspended by executing **kill -18 333** then it is required to be activated by ___________

343. **jobs command is available in ___________ shell**

344. ___________ **signal will be sent a foreground process when you press ctrl-c**

345. **Jobs** are supported in ___________ Shell.

346. In **C shell** a set of commands are ___________ they will be executed in sub shell.

347. **x = /home/nbv/raju.c; echo $x:t** displays ___________

348. In **Bourne shell set -a** ___________

349. **C shells** analogue to **command 1> file 2> errs** is ___________

350. In C shell **arithmetic's** are internal where as Bourne shell arithmetic's are ___________

351. **ELF** format means ___________

352. In C shell, **x = /home/nbv/raju.c; echo $x:t** displays raju.c. Its **equivalent in Bourne shell** is ___________

353. When **clri** command is used to clear inode of a file that file information is available in ___________

354. In tcsh ___________ command can be used to change the prompt to have path of current directory.

355. When a file system is mounted on a directory, the files previously present in the directory ___________ accessible.

356. ___________ and ___________ are pattern scanning and processing language.

357. The startup instructions for user's account can be kept in ___________ file

358. A file is displayed with line numbers using ___________ command.

359. ___________ contains instructions to locate executable code of UNIX.

360. ___________ file is used to give message to any user at the time of logging.

361. ___________ is the internal name of the file.

362. ___________ command can be used to resume a suspended process.

363. Default output format for numbers in awk is ___________

364. **Stateless** network is ___________

365.   **tdemon** is used in __________

366.   **uucico** means __________

367.   **Fully qualified domain name** is limited to __________ octets.

368.   **rsh** is used __________ TCP connections

369.   __________ is a piece of data that the client will use to identify the file system to the server whenever any further access is required.

370.   In UNIX, __________ is the **end of line character** in text files.

371.   **ls** is external command and **cd** is __________

372.   The **maximum number of files** (including directories) that a file system can hold is controlled by __________

373.   __________ command can be used to bring **current background job** to foreground.

374.   Both login Korn and Bourne shells uses __________ file.

375.   Quantum in UNIX is __________

376.   Bootstrapping is __________

377.   Exceptions are handled by __________ on behalf of process.

378.   Processors supports different execution modes for the sake of __________

379.   Mode switch means __________

380.   Swapper and pagedeamon are created during __________

381.   Super user GID is __________

382.   Software interrupts are called as __________

383.   __________ contains addresses of low-level routines that handle interrupts.

384.   In UNIX systems, the process priority is determined by __________

385.   Copy-on-Write means __________

386.   Entry point is __________

387.   A.out format header is __________ bytes

388.   The number of ticks per second, HZ us defined in __________ file

389.   **Resolvers** are programs that __________

True or False Questions

1. Tilde (~) in **C shell** when used alone refers to users home shell.   **Yes** (   ) **No** (   )

2. If tilde (~) in filename it will be always expanded by **C shell**.   **Yes** (   ) **No** (   )

3. **!!d** at the command line executes previous command after appending d at the end to previous command in both **C & Bourne** shells.   **Yes** (   ) **No** (   )

4. Does the following command work in C shell.   **Yes** (   ) **No** (   )

    set m = `my mam is`; echo \$a[*].

5. **Set m='my mam is'; echo \$a[*]** displays my mam is   **Yes** (   ) **No** (   )

6. All shell variables are available to child process.   **Yes** (   ) **No** (   )

7. A shell variable which is defined and exported in sub-shell are available in parent shell also.   **Yes** (   ) **No** (   )

8. Is the output of **echo \$history** is same in both **C & bash shells**.   **Yes** (   ) **No** (   )

9. **echo \$path[*]** gives value of path environment variable.   **Yes** (   ) **No** (   )

10. Du -sbx `ls -F | grep /` | sort –n   will show the size of the subdirectories of the current directory.   **Yes** (   ) **No** (   )

11. In C shell does the following commands produce same output.   **Yes** (   ) **No** (   )

    echo \$path

    echo \$path[*]

12. In **C shell, echo \$path*** gives list of directories   which **path** variable pointing.   **Yes** (   ) **No** (   )

13. Do you have freedom to set no of commands to be remembered in bash at command line (such as history = number)?.   **Yes** (   ) **No** (   )

14. In C shell once if you run **set time = 0, then for all the following commands time details will be printed. Is there any similar one step command in Bourne shell.**   **Yes** (   ) **No** (   )

15. **shift** in **C shell** works for only argv shell variable.   **Yes** (   ) **No** (   )

16. Does **C shell** distinguish EOF & EOL separately.   **Yes** (   ) **No** (   )

17. **set ignore EOF** makes **C shell** not to logout by entering ^d.   **Yes** (   ) **No** (   )

18. **set noglob** makes **C shell** to ignore file name expansion phase in   command execution.   **Yes** (   ) **No** (   )

19. Does the following two compound statements produce same result?.
    (a) **set date = 'date'; echo $#date** (b) **set date = `date`; echo $#date.**   **Yes** ( ) **No** ( )
20. Does the following two compound statements produce same result?.
    (a) **set date ='date'; echo $#date** (b) **set date="date"; echo $#date.**   **Yes** ( ) **No** ( )
21. In C shell **$?name** will display one or zero depends on shell variable name is defined
    or not.   **Yes** ( ) **No** ( )
22. **set noclobber** command in **C shell** abandons all redirection to file. **Yes** ( ) **No** ( )
23. **Bourne shell** does not expand files named by redirection directives.   **Yes** ( ) **No** ( )
24. **++, --** operators similar to c language can be used in Bourne shell.   **Yes** ( ) **No** ( )
25. **pushd** command without arguments changes top two directory names on
                                                                             Yes ( ) **No** ( )
26. When path is changed with **set** command, the **C shell** reconstructs its hash   table?.
                                                                             Yes ( ) **No** ( )
27. **unhash** disables **C shells** use of hash table.   **Yes** ( ) **No** ( )
28. **onintr** command without argument makes turn interrupts back on. **Yes** ( ) **No** ( )
29. **onintr ~** command turnoff all interrupts.   **Yes** ( ) **No** ( )
30. **onintr label** tells the shell where to transfers control when on interrupts occurs.
                                                                             Yes ( ) **No** ( )
31. Variable in **C shell** whose values are set are available to child process.
                                                                             Yes ( ) **No** ( )
32. Variable in **C shell** whose values are **setenv** are available to child process.
                                                                             Yes ( ) **No** ( )
33. **unsetenv** variable is exclusive to C shell only.   **Yes** ( ) **No** ( )
34. In **DOS dir** is internal command; similarly **ls** is UNIX internal command?.
                                                                             Yes ( ) **No** ( )
35. While executing shell internal command, shell does not start a separate process.
                                                                             Yes ( ) **No** ( )
36. Is it possible in UNIX a file name to consists / character?.   **Yes** ( ) **No** ( )
37. No. of **i-nodes** control the maximum no. of files you can create in a file system.
                                                                             Yes ( ) **No** ( )
38. Is it possible to change number of **i-nodes** without disturbing file system?.
                                                                             Yes ( ) **No** ( )
39. When you start **sub-shell** (Bourne), **sub-shell** does not read **.profile**.
                                                                             Yes ( ) **No** ( )
40. If you set path shell variable in **C shell**, automatically environment   variable **PATH**
    will be also set.   **Yes** ( ) **No** ( )
41. **notify** variable asks to inform you when a background job finishes. **Yes** ( ) **No** ( )

42. **Daemon** process will be "**sleeping**" till something to happen to deal with.

    Yes ( ) **No** ( )

43. When **kernel panic** message appears, kernels shuts the system down before any change to happen?.
    Yes ( ) **No** ( )

44. Background process (&) is a command which is no longer attached to a terminal.

    Yes ( ) **No** ( )

45. Bootstrap program is available in boot block.   **Yes** ( ) **No** ( )

46. Value of **file pointer** points next byte to read or write in a file.   **Yes** ( ) **No** ( )

47. Both **getc** and **fgetc** are macros which are defined in *stdio.h*.   **Yes** ( ) **No** ( )

48. **fgetc** and **fputc** are functions.   **Yes** ( ) **No** ( )

49. **I-list** and **i-number** are same.   **Yes** ( ) **No** ( )

50. **Core dump** is a file which will be created when a program is abnormally terminated.   **Yes** ( ) **No** ( )

51. **Job** and **process** are same.   **Yes** ( ) **No** ( )

52. **Job number** and **process ID (PID)'s** are same.   **Yes** ( ) **No** ( )

53. **Kernel** is the set of **system calls** and the **internal algorithms** that implements them.
    Yes ( ) **No** ( )

54. All system calls **return -1** when they fail.   **Yes** ( ) **No** ( )

55. If command includes path (absolute or relative), shell will not use PATH variable information.   **Yes** ( ) **No** ( )

56. **ls -l | grep '^.......rw'** , lists files which others can read and write. **Yes** ( ) **No** ( )

57. **awk** is very flexible than **sed** for text manipulation.   **Yes** ( ) **No** ( )

58. Efficiency of a program is inversely proportional to the no of **system calls** and amount of data transferred.   **Yes** ( ) **No** ( )

59. If offset and reference argument combination makes **lseek** system to fail then the file pointer will not change.   **Yes** ( ) **No** ( )

60. Using **lseek** we can change **file pointers** for terminal device.   **Yes** ( ) **No** ( )

61. **dup system** call duplicates an open file descriptor and returns new file descriptor.
    Yes ( ) **No** ( )

62. Can we link files across file systems using symbolic links?.   **Yes** ( ) **No** ( )

63. **C shell** executes commands defined in an alias without first creating a new copy of the shell.   **Yes** ( ) **No** ( )

64. **un-alias** command is used to break relationship between its argument and set of words defined with it with alias command.   **Yes** ( ) **No** ( )

65. In **Bourne shell**, while defining and assigning a value to a shell variable no blank spaces should be used on either side of =.   **Yes** ( ) **No** ( )

66. In **C shell**, while defining and assigning a value to a shell variable no blank spaces should be used on either side of =.   **Yes** ( ) **No** ( )

67. **Command language** programs are usually interpreted by the command language processor .   Yes ( ) No ( )

68. **ls -l|sed 1d|wc -l** command displays _____________   Yes ( ) No ( )

69. Does the following command produce same results.   Yes ( ) No ( )
    ls -l|sed 1d|wc -l
    ls -l|tail +2|wc -l

70. **ls -l|awk '/username/{k++} END{print k}'** outputs no. of files in P.W.D of a particular user (username).   Yes ( ) No ( )

71. **Difference** between modes of **executable shell file** and **executable binary file** is that shell script should have both read and execution permissions.   Yes ( ) No ( )

72. Is it possible to **open file through vi** if it has only "wx" permissions. Yes ( ) No ( )

73. **MAILCHECK** tells shell how often (seconds) it has to check for arrival of a new mail.   Yes ( ) No ( )

74. **awk variables** has to be explicitly declared, initialized before their use.

                                                          Yes ( ) No ( )

75. **cut** command can be used to divide the file into two files one with a set of lines the other with remaining.   Yes ( ) No ( )

76. **File descriptor** is an integer where as a file pointer is a pointer   to a structure.

                                                          Yes ( ) No ( )

77. In a file **i-node**, file name will not be seen.   Yes ( ) No ( )

78. "**chmod +t executable filename** " makes the program once executed   it will not be out of the swap device.   Yes ( ) No ( )

79. Once you change ownership of a file, it can be reversed again   only by you.

                                                          Yes ( ) No ( )

80. **pg** command has facility to check for a pattern in a file in both directions.

                                                          Yes ( ) No ( )

81. **more** command has facility to check for a pattern in a file in both directions.

                                                          Yes ( ) No ( )

82. **-f1-5** option with **cut** command displays information between 1 to 5 fields of input file of each line.   Yes ( ) No ( )

83. **cut** and **paste** are same.   Yes ( ) No ( )

84. **paste** can be used to paste files horizontally.   Yes ( ) No ( )

85. **take** is used to copy files from remote machine to local while working with **cu** command.   Yes ( ) No ( )

86. **CURSES** is a library of C functions to handle screen.   Yes ( ) No ( )

87. **trace** and **profile** commands are same.   Yes ( ) No ( )

88. When terminal Shell receives the SIGINT signal it terminates.   Yes ( ) No ( )

89. **SIGFPE** is signal sent by the Kernel to a process where floating point exception occurs.   Yes ( ) No ( )

90. **SIGSYS** indicates irrecoverable error in system call. Yes ( ) No ( )
91. While executing a pipe a temporary file in /tmp directory is created. Yes ( )No ( )
92. **Named pipe** is also called FIFO, is a pipe which uses permanent UNIX file.
    Yes ( ) No ( )
93. **mknod** command can be used to create device files and FIFO's.
    Yes ( ) No ( )
94. **mknod np p** command creates a named pipe np in P.W.D. Yes ( ) No ( )
95. **Difference** between | (**pipe**) and > (**output redirection**) is that > sends output to a file where as pipe will send to another process. Yes ( ) No ( )
96. In **UNIX** operating system widely used **GUI** is **X Windows**. Yes ( ) No ( )
97. **Kermit** is communication sw. Yes ( ) No ( )
98. **UNIX** gives equal-time-slices to all programs running in memory. Yes ( ) No ( )
99. **File encryption** is for maintaining privacy to the files. Yes ( ) No ( )
100. Without shell can we work after logging remotely into a UNIX machine.
    Yes ( ) No ( )
101. **grep** stands for globally searches a regular expression and print it. Yes ( ) No ( )
102. **4/8 port** is used in UNIX to connect dumb terminals. Yes ( ) No ( )
103. Any user having access to UNIX system automatically gets access to all files in it.
    Yes ( ) No ( )
104. In a typical UNIX OS there are several Kernels and one shell be running.
    Yes ( ) No ( )
105. **Password aging** is used to control hackers. Yes ( ) No ( )
106. **touch** command is used to create empty files.
107. Can we change name of a directory (with out physically moving files in it) in UNIX with mv command. Yes ( ) No ( )
108. Is it possible to create hidden directories. Yes ( ) No ( )
109. In the output of "**ls -l**" command if first column characters is m then the file is shared memory file. Yes ( ) No ( )
110. **undelete** command is not existing in UNIX. Yes ( ) No ( )
111. If for a file all the permissions are available for group, then any member of that group can change its permissions. Yes ( ) No ( )
112. If you have only execute permissions for a directory, can you find what files are in it ?. Yes ( ) No ( )
113. Is it possible to set sticky bit to a regular file?. Yes ( ) No ( )
114. **lc and lf** are variants of ls. Yes ( ) No ( )
115. **A terminal file** is always a block special file. Yes ( ) No ( )
116. **units** command converts quantities expressed in one scale to other. Yes ( ) No ( )

117. **umask** is UNIX file creation mask indicates what default permissions are assigned to a file when it is created.   **Yes ( ) No ( )**

118. **UNIX file system** is a **flat file** system.   **Yes ( ) No ( )**

119. **4.2 BSD** uses two block sizes in its file system .   **Yes ( ) No ( )**

120. During **disk formatting block** and **fragment sizes** are finalized.   **Yes ( ) No ( )**

121. If repeated transfer of large files are expected, block size should be high.   **Yes ( ) No ( )**

122. **I-node** of root directory of UNIX is located at a fixed place on disk.   **Yes ( ) No ( )**

123. One file is opened and closed still **i-node** of this file will be active and these are called **zombies**.   **Yes ( ) No ( )**

124. Is it possible to **split a file system between two hard disks**.   **Yes ( ) No ( )**

125. Smaller the **disk block** size larger the file access times.   **Yes ( ) No ( )**

126. **Internal fragmentation** increases with block size.   **Yes ( ) No ( )**

127. Does all file system partitions contains **boot block** (including bootable partition) ?.   **Yes ( ) No ( )**

128. An **allocated block** belongs to **only one file** in the file system.

129. If there are **no free data blocks on a file system,** OS stores the **rest of the file in data blocks of another file system**.   **Yes ( ) No ( )**

130. **File system inconsistency** can be said as mis-matching of **i-node** table entries in RAM and Hard Disk.   **Yes ( ) No ( )**

131. When you rename a file, new name will be associated to present **i-node**.   **Yes ( ) No ( )**

132. **I-node** numbers of a **symbolic name** is same as the actual files.   **Yes ( ) No ( )**

133. **df** space displays free space in megabytes.   **Yes ( ) No ( )**

134. **df and du** commands are same.   **Yes ( ) No ( )**

135. **ulimit** command can be executed only by super user.   **Yes ( ) No ( )**

136. **ulimit** can be changed by users.   **Yes ( ) No ( )**

137. If **you forget your password,** your system administrator can tell you.   **Yes ( ) No ( )**

138. If you enter list of names one after another after sort command at command prompt and terminated with CTRL + d, it will display all the names in alphabetical sequence.   **Yes ( ) No ( )**

139. **dd** command is for file conversion.   **Yes ( ) No ( )**

140. **compress** command always compresses the files content.   **Yes ( ) No ( )**

141. **zcat** is used to view compressed files, Where as to display last lines of a compressed file we can use **ztail**.   **Yes ( ) No ( )**

142. "<<" operator is used in shell programming.   **Yes** ( ) **No** ( )

143. Can we write input of **tee** command to more than one file?.   **Yes** ( ) **No** ( )

144. **bin** word is a reserved username.   **Yes** ( ) **No** ( )

145. If two users have **same password** then the encrypted string in /etc/passwd file is same?.   **Yes** ( ) **No** ( )

146. **Can there be more than one account with same name** on a UNIX system?.   **Yes** ( ) **No** ( )

147. **While entering password** cursor can not move at all.   **Yes** ( ) **No** ( )

148. Is there **any difference in the computers response** when one types wrong password and wrong username?.   **Yes** ( ) **No** ( )

149. **Stty** command indicates what are the erase and line kill characters are.   **Yes** ( ) **No** ( )

150. Is \c\a\l command is same as **cal** ?.   **Yes** ( ) **No** ( )

151. '**Who are you**' command is it available?.   **Yes** ( ) **No** ( )

152. What happens if set your erase character to '\' ?.   **Yes** ( ) **No** ( )

153. Can this command works **rm -r..** ?.   **Yes** ( ) **No** ( )

154. We can not have **hard link files** across two different file systems. **Yes** ( ) **No** ( )

155. **Symbolic links** permits to link files in two different file systems. **Yes** ( ) **No** ( )

156. Does a **symbolic link** file used any disk space (data blocks)?. **Yes** ( ) **No** ( )

157. **write** command replies weather the message successful or not. **Yes** ( ) **No** ( )

158. Communicating via **write** (simultaneously) can be said as asynchronous and full duplex.   **Yes** ( ) **No** ( )

159. If rama logged in more than one terminal, if you executes '**write rama**'command and write message on all the terminals message appears.   **Yes** ( ) **No** ( )

160. '**mesg n**' turns off write permission for other users.   **Yes** ( ) **No** ( )

161. **Permission modes of a terminal device file** will be reset for each login session.   **Yes** ( ) **No** ( )

162. **Can we stop super user** to send some message through write.   **Yes** ( ) **No** ( )

163. **wall** command can be used to send a message to all users.   **Yes** ( ) **No** ( )

164. **ls /usr/abc/nov/*** works?.   **Yes** ( ) **No** ( )

165. `**set prompt = \!\%**` command in C shell displays line numbers before the prompt.   **Yes** ( ) **No** ( )

166. **repeat 10 echo "who are you"** will display "who are you" message ten times.   **Yes** ( ) **No** ( )

167. In **awk**, variables have to be explicitly declared, initialized before their use.   **Yes** ( ) **No** ( )

168. **cut** command can be used to divide the file into two files one with a set of lines and the other with remaining.   Yes ( ) No ( )

169. **File descriptors** and file pointers are same.   Yes ( ) No ( )

170. In a files, **i-node** data structure its name will not be seen.   Yes ( ) No ( )

171. **Program, Process, and tasks** are synonymous.   Yes ( ) No ( )

172. **vrand** is for virtual memory handler.   Yes ( ) No ( )

173. **/etc/cron** file can not be executed by users except super user.   Yes ( ) No ( )

174. **write** uses TCP/IP protocol in exchange information between two users.

                                                                         Yes ( ) No ( )

175. **Can any user broadcast** and succeed in displaying a message on all terminals under any situation? .   Yes ( ) No ( )

176. In **C shell,** We can move foreground execution to background?.   Yes ( ) No ( )

177. Is `S1 = ABC S2 = XYZ` an acceptable shell variable assignment? Yes ( ) No ( )

178. Is it possible to declare and **initialize two shell variables along the command line separated with space.**   Yes ( ) No ( )

179. Does **a variable whose value is null** considered in shell command?.

                                                                         Yes ( ) No ( )

180. `unset PS1` is an acceptable command.   Yes ( ) No ( )

181. Is it possible to **assign a value to a positional parameter** (ex. $1 = 131)?.

                                                                         Yes ( ) No ( )

182. "Text file is busy" error message will appear if a program is running and you try to recompile its source code.   Yes ( ) No ( )

183. In a UNIX system with multiple partitions, **boot program** will located in the zero'th block of the hard disk.   Yes ( ) No ( )

184. In **system maintenance mode**, only one user can work.   Yes ( ) No ( )

185. **mtab or fstab** files contains information about file systems to be mounted.

                                                                         Yes ( ) No ( )

186. **As a root if you change, username (only) of a user,** then all the files of this users ownership also changed.   Yes ( ) No ( )

187. **NOLOGIN** in second field of a line in **/etc/passwd** field indicates that no ordinary user can login as that account.   Yes ( ) No ( )

188. **Can we add a user** to a group by changing **/etc/group** file.   Yes ( ) No ( )

189. Is it possible to **set password for group also.**   Yes ( ) No ( )

190. Is there any meaning for **execution permission of a device file** . Yes ( ) No ( )

191. **Total no. of physical files and directories** which can be created on file system is controlled by no of **i-node**s.   Yes ( ) No ( )

192. If you **mount a drive on to an existing directory** a previous files still can be accessed.   Yes ( ) No ( )

193. Variable declared in a shell can be displayed at dollar prompt using set command.

     Yes ( ) No ( )

194. Does **all UNIX file systems** contains **lost+found** directory.   **Yes ( ) No ( )**

195. A **user can not change his password as his username**, but root can do this for a user.   **Yes ( ) No ( )**

196. **Arithmetic expressions** will be **executed in shell** from left to right.

     Yes ( ) No ( )

197. Is it possible to assign **same home directory more than one user**?.

     Yes ( ) No ( )

198. In **any line error occurs,   does shell program continues** execution ?.

     Yes ( ) No ( )

199. All shell scripts **automatically set executed** in current shell.   **Yes ( ) No ( )**

200. If value of **OPTIND** is greater then $# arguments are correctly specified.

     Yes ( ) No ( )

201. **export** command displays list of environment variable which all exported in current shell only not inherited ones.   **Yes ( ) No ( )**

202. If an **exported variable** is changed in sub-shell,   then it has to be exported   again to see the modification in sub-shell.   **Yes ( ) No ( )**

203. If an **exported variable** is changed in sub-shell,   then it has to be exported again to see the modification in sub-shell except last parent shell.   **Yes ( ) No ( )**

204. **eval** command executes the command after all shell substitutions. **Yes ( ) No ( )**

205. A shell variable name and value can not consists of **meta characters**.

     Yes ( ) No ( )

206. Neither exported variable can **unset** nor **readonly variable** can be exported.

     Yes ( ) No ( )

207. UNIX is **immune against viruses and worms.**   **Yes ( ) No ( )**

208. **Shell viruses** are more dangerous than machine-language viruses. **Yes ( ) No ( )**

209. **"chmod -R go-w . "** command makes all the files in P.W.D recursively will such that they are not writable by others.   **Yes ( ) No ( )**

210. **find . -exec chmod go-w {} \;** makes group and others will not have write permissions to present working directory recursively for P.W.D.   **Yes ( ) No ( )**

211. **last** command displays usernames, ttyname, login times of most recent login to least recent.   **Yes ( ) No ( )**

212. ACL (Access Control lists) are used to specify file permissions.   **Yes ( ) No ( )**

213. chmod command specify which permissions should be on,   where as umask value is used to specify which permissions should be off.   **Yes ( ) No ( )**

214. Is it **possible to delete others files in /tmp** directory by a user.   **Yes ( ) No ( )**

215. To find file names in the entire system whose **set-group-id**'s are set, we can use
     find / -type f -a -perm -2000 –print   **Yes ( ) No ( )**

216. Setting **setuid bit** of system commands allows ordinary users to use   them in a limited manner.   **Yes ( ) No ( )**

217. In **block special file** does a block can be read randomly ?.   **Yes ( ) No ( )**

218. Does **creation of socket returns a file descriptor** ?.   **Yes ( ) No ( )**

219. **Sockets** are used to communicate to processes working on different machines ?.
                                                              Yes ( ) No ( )

220. When UNIX shell starts a process,   it puts copies of its environment variable on the **process stack**. if this process should later fork, will the child automatically get these variable too ?.   **Yes ( ) No ( )**

221. It is impossible for a **process to send a signal** to another process that is not in the group.   **Yes ( ) No ( )**

222. **I-lists** and **c-lists** are same.   **Yes ( ) No ( )**

223. **C-lists** are used to buffer characters from character devices before they will be handled to process?.   **Yes ( ) No ( )**

224. **Locks** are used to avoid **racing condition** while two or more processes are using same file at the same time.   **Yes ( ) No ( )**

225. Does **i-node** of a file contain any information about path of the file. **Yes ( ) No ( )**

226. Whenever a file is changed, then its **i-node** and file contents will be changed.
                                                              Yes ( ) No ( )

227. Whenever **i-node** information changes; file contents also changes. **Yes ( ) No ( )**

228. Whenever **a file system is created .** of root directory will be initialized to root **i-node**.
                                                              Yes ( ) No ( )

229. When-ever an entry is removed from a directory, then the **i-node** entry will be made to zero in the respective directory block.   **Yes ( ) No ( )**

230. **ch eroot** system call is used change a process notion of the file system root.
                                                              Yes ( ) No ( )

231. Whenever a file is created, then the information in super block, i.e. next free **i-node** number is assigned to this file.   **Yes ( ) No ( )**

232. "Remembered **i-node**" is the one in super block which is unassigned
                                                              Yes ( ) No ( )

233. When **quoted** C shell does not recognize special characters as separated   words when they are quoted.   **Yes ( ) No ( )**

234. **C shell** makes an entry in an internal table that relates the all the executable files in the directories specified by PATH variable. **Yes ( ) No ( )**

235. Commands in **.cshrc** and **.login** will be executed in sequence at login time.
                                                              Yes ( ) No ( )

236. **stty** command can be used in vi editor to set key definitions.   **Yes ( ) No ( )**

237. If a directory is writable then **files can be removed** irrespective of their permissions.

     Yes (   ) **No** (   )

238. If file (f1) is **symbolically linked** to file f2, then is it possible to   access content of file f2 after executing "**mv f2 f3**" command ?   **Yes** (   ) **No** (   )

239. Is it possible to make one directory to be **spread across more than one file system** ?.

     Yes (   ) **No** (   )

240. Does the output of **echo $PATH and $path** is same in both bash and C shells ?

     Yes (   ) **No** (   )

241. **Can we link symbolic file with another symbolic file** and if the first symbolic file is removed can we access original file?.   **Yes** (   ) **No** (   )

242. If file aa is hard linked via a file aaa and aaa is hard linked via   aaaa then can we access aa after removing aaa file ?   **Yes** (   ) **No** (   )

243. **od** command is used to display all the characters of a file with their ASCII code in octal system   **Yes** (   ) **No** (   )

244. **File** command infers from the file name extension, type of the file. **Yes** (   ) **No** (   )

245. In any UNIX (like) system, executable files will have **octal value 410**   as magic number at the beginning.   **Yes** (   ) **No** (   )

246. When-ever a **text file** is created using an editor it also adds a special **magic number** at the beginning of file   **Yes** (   ) **No** (   )

247. For a **device file,**   its **i-node** contains **i-list** of disk block numbers. **Yes** (   ) **No** (   )

248. For a **device file,**   its **i-node** contains internal name of the device. **Yes** (   ) **No** (   )

249. Is **who >..** command acceptable.   **Yes** (   ) **No** (   )

250. Directories in an UNIX file also conceived as ordinary files. So is it possible to **ed** to add files to it? .   **Yes** (   ) **No** (   )

251. **du | awk '{ print $2 $1 }'** command displays listing of files along with their disk consumption .   **Yes** (   ) **No** (   )

252. Is it possible to have **to users** (with different usernames) to have **same UID** ?.

     Yes (   ) **No** (   )

253. **fg** command is used to bring current background job to foreground.

     Yes (   ) **No** (   )

254. Is it possible to give **interactive input to a program which is running in background** ?.   **Yes** (   ) **No** (   )

255. **jobs** command lists all the background jobs.   **Yes** (   ) **No** (   )

256. **Zombies** are dead processes which are not deleted from process table.

     Yes (   ) **No** (   )

257. **Does zombies** consume any **system resources**?.   **Yes** (   ) **No** (   )

258. Does **zombies** displays after **reboot**?.   **Yes** (   ) **No** (   )

259. Interactive commands such as **vi** will use **shell as interpreter.**   **Yes** (   ) **No** (   )

260. **NIS** stands for Network Information service.   **Yes ( ) No ( )**

261. **NFS** stands for Network File system.   **Yes ( ) No ( )**

262. **Grep '^\.XX' filename** displays those lines of file which starts with **.XX** pattern.

     Yes ( ) No ( )

263. If abc is a shell script file then **. abc** at the $ prompt takes some arguments.

     Yes ( ) No ( )

264. Output of **echo */*** in the directory / is same as the command **ls -lR /**

     Yes ( ) No ( )

265. **goto statement** is not available in shell programs.   **Yes ( ) No ( )**

266. Unlike C and DOS batch programs, **shell script does not have any label** facility to change program control.   **Yes ( ) No ( )**

267. Can we create file A using the following sequence of commands. **umask 777; cat > A**

     Yes ( ) No ( )

268. If **umask** is set to **777** then is it possible to edit **existing file through** vi editor?

     Yes ( ) No ( )

269. If you had a file with **permissions 666** in a directory with **permissions 755** then any one can search and change the file?.   **Yes ( ) No ( )**

270. If you have a **722** to a directory /home/guest and you are neither owner of the directory or super user, can you goto that directory and create a file using cat?.

     Yes ( ) No ( )

271. Is the output of the following two commands are same?.   **Yes ( ) No ( )**

     1. echo`echo \`date\``

     2. echo`date`

272. Does the following two commands behave similarly?.   **Yes ( ) No ( )**

     `ls`

     ls

273. Does the output of the following command display a line containing abc?.

     ls -l >abc; cat abc (note abc file does not exist initially)   **Yes ( ) No ( )**

274. Does the output of the following command sequences is same.

     ls -l >abc; cat abc   **Yes ( ) No ( )**

     ls -l | tee abc

275. Does the following commands works similarly?   **Yes ( ) No ( )**

     cat abc >xyz

     cat abc 1>xyz

276. Does the following commands gives the same result.   **Yes ( ) No ( )**

     cat abc xyz 2>pqr 1>&2

     cat abc xyz >pqr 2>&1

     (note xyz file is not existing)

277. **nice command** can be used by a user to increase priority of his process.

Yes ( ) No ( )

278. Files created using **split** are ASCII text files which are editable.   Yes ( ) No ( )

279. **Shell variable if exported** will be **inheritable** by sub-shells.   Yes ( ) No ( )

280. An **exported shell variable defined in a sub-shell** is available in its **parents shell** even after sub-shell dies.   Yes ( ) No ( )

281. An **environment variable when modified in a sub-shell** those modifications will be seen in parent shell also.   Yes ( ) No ( )

282. A **device controls** only one physical device of a given type.   Yes ( ) No ( )

283. **Software devices** will always have an **associated physical device**. Yes ( ) No ( )

284. **cpio** can be used to copy directories from one partition to others.   Yes ( ) No ( )

285. **find . -print |cpio -pd /mnt/ram**   command moves all files of P.W.D   to the directory /mnt/ram recursively.   Yes ( ) No ( )

286. **find / -cpio /dev/rmt0 -print > /tmp/log**   command copies entire root (/) file system onto magnetic tape.   Yes ( ) No ( )

287. Does a **group has any password** in UNIX.   Yes ( ) No ( )

288. **chmod 4000 filename** acceptable?.   Yes ( ) No ( )

289. "**chmod 4000 filename**" command sets user-id bit of a file to user who executes the same.   Yes ( ) No ( )

290. "**chmod 2000 filename**" sets group-id as owner of the actual file when it is executed.

Yes ( ) No ( )

291. "**chmod 1000 filename**" sets sticky-bit to the file.   Yes ( ) No ( )

292. **UNIX system V** uses disk block sizes as 1024 bytes.   Yes ( ) No ( )

293. **mkfs** automatically selects number of **i-node** blocks.   Yes ( ) No ( )

294. '**Device busy**' error message indicates you are trying to unmount a file system which you presently working in.   Yes ( ) No ( )

295. **cc** command copies and also links.   Yes ( ) No ( )

296. **ar t /lib/libc.a** displays what functions are in the archive.   Yes ( ) No ( )

297. **cxref** is used to display variable and procedure names which are called in a set of c programs.   Yes ( ) No ( )

298. **cflow** is used to display program flow (which procedures are being called).

Yes ( ) No ( )

299. **Compiler** and **link-editor** are same.   Yes ( ) No ( )

300. In compiling C programs, only one error will be displayed for each of the line with error(s).   Yes ( ) No ( )

301. When you use **-C option** does linkage editor will be executed?.   Yes ( ) No ( )

302. **find /tmp -mtime +2 -exec rm {}\;** command removes files in /tmp directory which are not modified for 2 days.   Yes ( ) No ( )

303. **find $HOME -atime +10 -ok cat {} \;** displays files which are accessed since last 10 days.   Yes (   ) No (   )

304. **find /home/venkat -print | cpio -o > /dev/rmt** makes all the files under venkat directory to magnetic tape.   Yes (   ) No (   )

305. Through **cpio** files will be dumped along with full path.   Yes (   ) No (   )

306. **cpio -o </dev/rmt0** makes files to copy from tape to their original location.
                                                                   Yes (   ) No (   )

307. **access()** and **chdir()** functions are same.   Yes (   ) No (   )

308. In specifying **wild-cards** as **[1-30]** is same as **[0-3]**?.   Yes (   ) No (   )

309. A file contains hyphen as its first character, can we modify using vi editor.
                                                                   Yes (   ) No (   )

310. **P.W.D** command is also used to check password.   Yes (   ) No (   )

311. **cc in UNIX** is a C compiler.   Yes (   ) No (   )

312. **'rm'** cannot remove directories.   Yes (   ) No (   )

313. **'spell'** returns correctly spelled words.   Yes (   ) No (   )

314. **'stop'** command is used to halt the process.   Yes (   ) No (   )

315. **UNIX** has **Ctrl+Z** as **EOF** marker.   Yes (   ) No (   )

316. **awk** is a programming language.   Yes (   ) No (   )

317. **system calls** use library functions.   Yes (   ) No (   )

318. **Super user** can force any user to change his password.   Yes (   ) No (   )

319. **ls -d** lists all the directories in the current directory. Yes (   ) No (   )

320. **Kernel stack** is empty when process executes in user mode. Yes (   ) No (   )

321. **UNIX Kernel** (version prior to SVR 4.2) is fully **preemptable,** i.e,   processes running in kernel can be preempted.   Yes (   ) No (   )

322. Unlike DOS,   **UNIX is a Client server Model** Operating System where the kernel runs as a separate set of processes performing resource management services to user processes.   Yes (   ) No (   )

323. In **ufs file system** there are **multiple copies of SUPER BLOCK.** Yes (   ) No (   )

324. In **UNIX devices** are treated as files.   Yes (   ) No (   )

325. The execution of **ln** command internally results in the allocation of new **i-node**.
                                                                   Yes (   ) No (   )

326. In **awk, BEGIN** is the first routine to be executed after the input is read.
                                                                   Yes (   ) No (   )

327. **sed** is a non interactive stream oriented editor.   Yes (   ) No (   )

328. In shell, the variable **$$** represents **process id of last command started in background.**   Yes (   ) No (   )

329. **umask** command is used to mask signals.   Yes (   ) No (   )

330. When a **file system is mounted on a directory** the files previously in the directory cannot be accessed. Yes ( ) No ( )

331. **Super user** can write to a file even if file doesn't has write permissions. Yes ( ) No ( )

332. **i-node** is never locked across a system call. Yes ( ) No ( )

333. If a directory does not has execute permissions you cannot create a file in it. Yes ( ) No ( )

334. By pressing **ZZ** one can save a file in vi editor. Yes ( ) No ( )

335. **cmp f1 f2,** prints location of 1st difference in two files. Yes ( ) No ( )

336. **ls -t** lists the files in time order, with most recent first. Yes ( ) No ( )

337. **who|wc -l** tells number of users currently logged in machine. Yes ( ) No ( )

338. When a **ln** command is executed, another physical copy of file is not created. Yes ( ) No ( )

339. **p1&&p2** means if p1 is successful then p2 will be executed. Yes ( ) No ( )

340. **tcsh** stands for terminal based C shell. Yes ( ) No ( )

341. **tcsh** supports automatic logout after an extended idle period. Yes ( ) No ( )

342. **Jsh** is a version of bash which includes C shell style job control. Yes ( ) No ( )

343. **msh** (MH shell) is developed Rand Co. allows to instant access of e-mail. Yes ( ) No ( )

344. **r** command in **korn shell** allows you to execute previous command. Yes ( ) No ( )

345. If one gives a command line argument for **r command in korn shell** then most recent command which starts with the specified command line argument will be executed. Yes ( ) No ( )

346. **Kernel** is the most essential (vital) part of the OS which is required to be loaded into memory first. Yes ( ) No ( )

347. Does the command **ls d[oa]d** lists the file **doad**?. Yes ( ) No ( )

348. ***[10-99]** denotes files which ends with 2 digits between 10 and 99. Yes ( ) No ( )

349. ***[a-z]*[a-z]*** wild card pattern matches all filenames with at least two lowercase characters. Yes ( ) No ( )

350. TO-DAY is a valid shell variable. Yes ( ) No ( )

351. **Month_salary** can be a valid value for a shell variable X. Yes ( ) No ( )

352. **PS1 = "proceed\?"** changes the prompt to proceed?. Yes ( ) No ( )

353. Does the **set** and **export** commands in bash produces same output if you executes them without any argument?. Yes ( ) No ( )

354. **B S D** Stands for Berkeley Software Distribution. Yes ( ) No ( )

355. When you press a **key**, a **signal is sent to host**, which in turn responds to display unit to display the character. Yes ( ) No ( )

356. If you press **CTRL + D** keys simultaneously, will you **logout always**?.

                                                      Yes ( ) **No** ( )

357. **Login** command allows the present user to logout and you will see again login prompt.   **Yes** ( ) **No** ( )

358. Does the following commands behaves same way?.   **Yes** ( ) **No** ( )
     rm   -fr ~/extra
     rm   -fr ~ /extra

359. **LINK** is the connection between a file name and its i-node.   **Yes** ( ) **No** ( )

360. **Hard links** cannot allow you to create a link to a directory.   **Yes** ( ) **No** ( )

361. **Hard links** is not possible between files in two different file systems.

                                                   Yes ( ) **No** ( )

362. **Soft links** can be made between files in two different file systems. **Yes** ( ) **No** ( )

363. **LOGIN SHELL** is the shell which automatically started whenever one login into system.   **Yes** ( ) **No** ( )

364. **chsh** command can be used to change default shell of a user by user himself.

                                                     Yes ( ) **No** ( )

365. **chsh** command should be executed by super user.   **Yes** ( ) **No** ( )

366. Does **chsh rao /bin/ksh** is valid command.   **Yes** ( ) **No** ( )

367. **File c** enables file name completion.   **Yes** ( ) **No** ( )

368. **echo $?** and **echo $status** does same thing.   **Yes** ( ) **No** ( )

369. If you **set ignored,** you can not logout using **^d**.   **Yes** ( ) **No** ( )

370. If a built in c shell variable is unset then its name will not appears by executing simple set command without any arguments.   **Yes** ( ) **No** ( )

371. **Term** and **TERM** are same.   **Yes** ( ) **No** ( )

372. **setenv TERM**   **Yes** ( ) **No** ( )
     printenv
     Both the commands works similarly.

373. Whenever you change built in shell variable (**home** or **term**) their environment variables HOME or TERM also gets charged; vice versa.   **Yes** ( ) **No** ( )

374. What happens if a shell scripts name is **same as echo**?. Does it executes by just simply typing **echo**?.   **Yes** ( ) **No** ( )

375. **init** directly interacts with HW without the help of Kernel.   **Yes** ( ) **No** ( )

376. **Context of a directory file** is created by Kernel.   **Yes** ( ) **No** ( )

377. Does the command **ls d[0a]d** lists the file **doad**?.   **Yes** ( ) **No** ( )

378. ***[10-99]** denotes files which ends with 2 digits between 10 to 99.   **Yes** ( ) **No** ( )

379. **pipes** are implemented through sockets in BSD based UNIX systems.

                                                   Yes ( ) **No** ( )

380. ***[a-z]*[a-z]*** Wild card pattern matches all filenames with at least two lower case characters. Yes ( ) No ( )

381. **TO-DAY** is a valid shell variable. Yes ( ) No ( )

382. **Month_salary** can be a valid value for a shell variable. Yes ( ) No ( )

383. **PS1="proceed \?"** changes the prompt to **proceed\?.** Yes ( ) No ( )

384. Does the **set** and **export** commands in bash produces same output if you execute them without any argument?. Yes ( ) No ( )

385. Normally shell prints one **prompt** after multiple commands. Yes ( ) No ( )

386. In the following command, **input** for **wc** is output of **who** only. Yes ( ) No ( )
date;who|wc

387. Both **ls *** and **echo *** displays same output. Yes ( ) No ( )

388. Does the following command produce same output?. Yes ( ) No ( )
ls .*
echo .*

389. Programs uses PATH variable information where as shell uses path variable information. Yes ( ) No ( )

390. **setenv PATH /bin:/usr/bin::/usr/local/bin** Yes ( ) No ( )
In the above command :: indicates current directory.

391. In C shell , **set prompt = 'RITCH \!\>'** changes prompt to display command number also. Yes ( ) No ( )

392. **-r** option with history command behaves similar to now -r works with sort command. Yes ( ) No ( )

393. **^xq^e** command replace string xq with e in previous comman and executes. Yes ( ) No ( )

394. **get -p s.main.c** would write the latest version of the source file stored in s.main.c to terminal. Yes ( ) No ( )

395. **prs** command is used to print information about an **sccs** file. Yes ( ) No ( )

396. Does **make** work together with **sccs**?. Yes ( ) No ( )

397. If there is a file **s.a.c** instead of **a.c** (which really **make** looking for), does **make** use **s.a.c**?. Yes ( ) No ( )

398. **su** command can be used change your use-id as some one else's. Yes ( ) No ( )

399. **newgrp** command allows to change your group. Yes ( ) No ( )

400. **cron** can be used to run program periodically. Yes ( ) No ( )

401. **trap** command is available only in C shell. Yes ( ) No ( )

402. Similar to any programming languages, shell programming also require compiling. Yes ( ) No ( )

403. The **Bourne shell** allows **exception handling** using the **trap** command. Yes ( ) No ( )

404. The **trap** command is not available in C shell.   Yes ( ) No ( )

405. **Bourne shell** uses test and expression utilities to evaluate conditional and arithmetic expression.   Yes ( ) No ( )

406. **C & Korn** shell directly evaluate expressions without test/expression.

    Yes ( ) No ( )

407. In Bourne shell if you start a process either in background or foreground it will be in same state till it complete.   Yes ( ) No ( )

408. **Virtual machine** runs on bare hardware.   Yes ( ) No ( )

409. In UNIX, **several processes** may be active at any one time.   Yes ( ) No ( )

410. Interpretation of **redirection '<' or '>'** is done by the executing program.

    Yes ( ) No ( )

411. **Grep** is example of filter.   Yes ( ) No ( )

412. **Environmental variables** are local variables.   Yes ( ) No ( )

413. **While or until loop** structure is preferred when some changing condition halts the loop.   Yes ( ) No ( )

414. **Testing** other than **equality of string** is possible through case statement.

    Yes ( ) No ( )

415. **Directory is treated as a file** in UNIX.   Yes ( ) No ( )

416. **Array subscript in awk** cannot be string of characters.   Yes ( ) No ( )

417. **Moving between** a **user mode** and **kernel mode** is known as context switching.

    Yes ( ) No ( )

418. It is possible to **write** a **message** when user is **not logged in**?.   Yes ( ) No ( )

419. We can **stop** your **group member** sending **message** to you by **chmod**.

    Yes ( ) No ( )

420. **MAILCHECK** is an environment variable which informs mail program to check your mail box at regular intervals.   Yes ( ) No ( )

421. **write** will interrupt receiving users work where as mail will not.   Yes ( ) No ( )

422. Can we **save information received from write in a file.**   Yes ( ) No ( )

423. Variables in a **shell does support integer, float**, etc.,.   Yes ( ) No ( )

424. When we **export a variable**, a copy of the variable is passed in to the shells created subsequently.   Yes ( ) No ( )

425. **Passing environment variables** to sub-shell is same as passing a variable to a function in C language by value.   Yes ( ) No ( )

426. **Kernel** is the most essential (vital) part of the OS which is required to be loaded into memory first. Yes ( ) No ( )

427. Does the output of the following commands are same?.

    (a) **ls x[^a-z]** (b) **ls x[!a-z]n** Yes ( ) No ( )

428. Does the output of the following commands are same?.

    (a) **ls x.z** (b) **ls xiz** Yes ( ) No ( )

429. Does the following expressions are same?.

    (a) **^$** (b) **^ *$** Yes ( ) No ( )

430. Regular expression **[+\-][0-9][0-9]** matches any two digit integer with a preceding - or +. Yes ( ) No ( )

431. Does the following command work in C shell?. Yes ( ) No ( )
    grep "ABC" xyz>pqr 2>lmn ?

432. **<<** is here document then **>>** there document. Yes ( ) No ( )

433. Does the following is acceptable field separator with **awk**?. Yes ( ) No ( )
    awk -F "xxx"

434. Does the following two **awk** commands work in the same manner?.
    awk -F "|" '/rao/' filename Yes ( ) No ( )
    awk -F "|" '/rao/ {print}' filename

435. Does the following two **awk** commands produce same result?. Yes ( ) No ( )
    awk -F "|" '{print}' filename
    awk -F "|" '{print $0}' filename

436. Does the following two commands produce same result?.
    awk '{print $1 $3}' filename
    awk '{print $1, $3}' filename

437. Do we require to put single quotes if you plan to put **awk** commands in a file and run the same with **awk -f** option? Yes ( ) No ( )

438. With **awk BEGIN** word opening **curly brace** should be on the same   line as that of BEGIN word. Yes ( ) No ( )

439. With **sort** command default alphabetical order and optional   dictionary order produce same results. Yes ( ) No ( )

440. **uniq** compares lines in a file whereas **comm** compare lines in two different files.
    Yes ( ) No ( )

441. Both **awk, ed** accepts command from a file. Yes ( ) No ( )

442. Is it possible to insert text into a file using **sed**?. Yes ( ) No ( )

443. **sed**'s main buffer is known as **pattern space**. Yes ( ) No ( )

444. **sed** read a line from the specified file and executes set of commands specified on that
      line before going to next line.   Yes ( ) No ( )

445. Does the following commands works similarly?.   Yes ( ) No ( )
      sed 's/xyz/XYZ/g' filename
      sed -e 's/xyz/XYZ/g' -e '/XYZ/q' filename

446. **!p** is if acceptable command in **sed**?.   Yes ( ) No ( )

447. Does the following commands produce same output?.   Yes ( ) No ( )
      cut -f1,8,3 filename
      awk '{print $1,$8,$3}' filename

448. Does the following produce same result?.   Yes ( ) No ( )
      cut -f 1,3,2 filename
      cut -f 3,1,2 filename

449. **paste** filename and cat filename commands behaves similarly.   Yes ( ) No ( )

450. **Paste** can receive a list of separator characters.   Yes ( ) No ( )

451. The **i-node list** generally occupies the first sector.   Yes ( ) No ( )

452. A file in **UNIX** is a stream **of** bytes.   Yes ( ) No ( )

453. **Major** and **Minor** numbers of a file identify the hardware link.   Yes ( ) No ( )

454. **split -20 test.c** will split the file test.c in blocks of 20.   Yes ( ) No ( )

455. If **var = haha** then the following execution **echo ${var?}** will print haha?.

                                                                   Yes ( ) No ( )

456. With the help of the **export** command we can export a variable along with its value
      from the parent shell to the child shell and vice versa.   Yes ( ) No ( )

457. The command **cut -d: f1,5 /etc/passwd** gives a list of user ID and names.

                                                                   Yes ( ) No ( )

458. The **i-node** number computing to a file can not be seen by user.   Yes ( ) No ( )

459. The **vi** editor is a line editor.   Yes ( ) No ( )

460. The file having **protection 466** can not be read by anybody other than user.

                                                                   Yes ( ) No ( )

461. Does the following are same in **Bourne shell**?.   Yes ( ) No ( )
      (a) **x =**
          test $x="MBA"
          echo $?
      (b) **x =**
          test "$x"="MBA"
          echo $?

462. Is the following is valid **Bourne shell** statement?.   Yes ( ) No ( )
      if ["x-y" -ne   "x+2"]

463. Is there **any option** like (**-r**) with test which can be used to find a file is a symbolic
      link or not?.   Yes ( ) No ( )

464. In **Korn shell** it is possible to check a file is **older** than another file. **Yes** ( ) **No** ( )

465. **test** command works for both numeric and string comparison whereas expr is not.

                                                              Yes ( ) **No** ( )

466. Does the following work similarly given i = 2?.   **Yes** ( ) **No** ( )

    (a) **echo `$i *  70`** (b) **echo `$i '*' 70`**

467. Does the following **two commands gives same results?.**   **Yes** ( ) **No** ( )

    (a) echo Enter $amount or * two see all the customers.

    (b) echo `Enter $amount or * two see all the customers`.

468. **Double quoting of strings** informs the shell to evaluate the string. **Yes** ( ) **No** ( )

469. The **substitution** on variable between double quotes is same as normal command-line substitution of a variable?   **Yes** ( ) **No** ( )

470. Does the following commands produce same results?.   **Yes** ( ) **No** ( )

    (a) **echo $xyz**   (b) **echo "$xyz"**

471. **Single quote** pair inside a double quote pair hide the single quote from shells evaluation.   **Yes** ( ) **No** ( )

472. **typeset -i** command in korn shell is used to make variables as integer type.

                                                              Yes ( ) **No** ( )

473. In C language * can be used as indirection operator to a pointer variable whereas * in korn shell is the array reference operator which displays all the defined elements of an array variable.   **Yes** ( ) **No** ( )

474. Does **IFS is available** in C shell?.   **Yes** ( ) **No** ( )

475. **sort + 0.20 –0.25 filename.**   **Yes** ( ) **No** ( )
    The above command is acceptable?.

476. Both **sed and grep commands** can accept complex searching commands from a file.

                                                              Yes ( ) **No** ( )

477. Both **sed awk grep commands** can accept complex searching commands from a file.

                                                              Yes ( ) **No** ( )

478. **Microsoft word, word perfect** are available for some UNIX systems also.

                                                              Yes ( ) **No** ( )

479. Both shell variable and C language variable names can start with_ **(underscore)** symbol.   **Yes** ( ) **No** ( )

480. **default** and **continue** statements are available in only in C shell.   **Yes** ( ) **No** ( )

481. Is there any command in Bourne shell which is equivalent to C shells **unsetenv** command?.   **Yes** ( ) **No** ( )

482. In both korn and C shells while assigning a value to a variable there should not be any space to both sides of =.   **Yes** ( ) **No** ( )

483. Does the following two statement sequences are same?.   Yes ( ) No ( )
     (a) ${AAA="xyz"} (b) if [!$AAA]
     then
         AAA=xyz
     fi

484. **Csplit** and **split** commands are exactly same.   Yes ( ) No ( )

485. In both korn and C shell, ls command produce same results?.   Yes ( ) No ( )

486. If you have a file xxx with permissions 400 (for you) and the directory in which that
     file is existing has writing permissions for you. If you try to delete this file what
     message will you get?.   Yes ( ) No ( )

487. **Line<filename** displays first line of the file.   Yes ( ) No ( )

488. Does the following command works?.   Yes ( ) No ( )
     grep -l export PATH *

489. **–i option** with **rm** and **grep** does the same task.   Yes ( ) No ( )

490. Does the following commands produce same output?.   Yes ( ) No ( )
     (a) **ls -a |paste - - - -** (b) **ls -a |paste -S -d "\t\t\t\n" -**

491. **ORS** (output record separator) is used in awk.   Yes ( ) No ( )

492. Does the following are exactly same?.   Yes ( ) No ( )
     (a) **(x1;x2)|wc**   (b) **{x1;x2}|wc**

493. Does the following command sequences are same?.   Yes ( ) No ( )
     (a) **xyz||{abc;x1}** (b) **xyz||abc;x1**

494. Does the following command sequences are same?.   Yes ( ) No ( )
     (a) **xyz||abc;x1** (b) **xyz**
     if [$? -Ne 0]
     then
      abc
     else
     x1
     fi

495. **File management** is the task of the shell in UNIX.   Yes ( ) No ( )

496. The **device drivers** are a part of the kernel in UNIX.   Yes ( ) No ( )

497. **Real time operating systems** should be batch processing system. Yes ( ) No ( )

498. A person who will write the kernel of an OS must have knowledge of the hardware.
                                                                   Yes ( ) No ( )

499. A user is willing to delete a file from the disk, he would directly interact with the
     kernel of the OS.   Yes ( ) No ( )

500. A **directory** is also a file in UNIX.   Yes ( ) No ( )

501. The **absolute path** of a file should start with the root.   Yes ( ) No ( )

502. The **directory** directly stores information about the **physical location** of the file.

     Yes ( ) No ( )

503. The **directory** directly stores information about the **protection** of the file.

     Yes ( ) No ( )

504. A directory having a single file can be deleted by **rmdir** command.

     Yes ( ) No ( )

505. One can delete a directory having only two entries to name . and .. can be removed by **rmdir** command.   **Yes ( ) No ( )**

506. The **rm -r** command can be used to delete a directory completely. **Yes ( ) No ( )**

507. The advantage of the **hierarchical file system** is that it consumes less space.

     Yes ( ) No ( )

508. UNIX makes a **distinction between the text and binary files**.   **Yes ( ) No ( )**

509. The command **rm xy*** removes all files that begin with xy from all directories.

     Yes ( ) No ( )

510. If there are no more readers and writers to a **pipe** does the pipe exists.

     Yes ( ) No ( )

511. The **more** command appends new lines to a file.   **Yes ( ) No ( )**

512. Pressing **y** in command mode   present word will be deleted in **vi** editor.

     Yes ( ) No ( )

513. A file edited through **vi** can be saved by pressing **ZZ.**   **Yes ( ) No ( )**

514. It is possible to **switch from vi to ed** by pressing Escape key.   **Yes ( ) No ( )**

515. An **i-node** is very special to a file.   **Yes ( ) No ( )**

516. An **i-node** is a special file.   **Yes ( ) No ( )**

517. The **device files are stored in /etc.**   **Yes ( ) No ( )**

518. We can see **details of a device file** with ls -l command.   **Yes ( ) No ( )**

519. A **disk is character oriented device.**   **Yes ( ) No ( )**

520. Always a **device file** can be either **character** or **block** oriented.   **Yes ( ) No ( )**

521. When we wanted to **install mouse** we can **execute /dev/mouse** command.

     Yes ( ) No ( )

522. We can **execute a device file** to access the same.   **Yes ( ) No ( )**

523. **I-node** information of a file can be used to track down the physical location of the file on disk.   **Yes ( ) No ( )**

524. A **physical file** in UNIX will be stored in continuous locations.   **Yes ( ) No ( )**

525. The **i-nodes** resides in disk.   **Yes ( ) No ( )**

526. The **maximum file size** is controlled by the **i-node size.**   Yes (   ) No (   )

527. Common **user can not see the i-node number of a file which he owns.**

                                                                              Yes (   ) No (   )

528. **cat** and **tee** commands are filters.   Yes (   ) No (   )

529. **more** is a filter.   Yes (   ) No (   )

530. The **test** command can be applied over strings and files but not on the numeric values.

                                                                              Yes (   ) No (   )

531. The **df** command displays what operating systems are installed on a disk.

                                                                              Yes (   ) No (   )

532. The **system calls** can be used by the users directly.

                                                                              Yes (   ) No (   )

533. **UNIX commands use the system calls** for their operation.

                                                                              Yes (   ) No (   )

534. **Access** system call can be used to know whether a file is read protected or not.

                                                                              Yes (   ) No (   )

535. **printf** is a system call.   Yes (   ) No (   )

536. **printf** is a library function.   Yes (   ) No (   )

537. **A jobs priority** can be increased by the owner of the job.   Yes (   ) No (   )

538. **Super user** can see the password of a user in /etc/passwd file whereas users can not
      do the same.   Yes (   ) No (   )

539. **Memory management** is done in UNIX by shell.   Yes (   ) No (   )

540. When a program is to be compiled the **user will have to make a kernel call.**

                                                                              Yes (   ) No (   )

541. **More than one process** can be active at any given time in UNIX even if only one
      processor is there.   Yes (   ) No (   )

542. A **background process will run a sub shell.**   Yes (   ) No (   )

543. If the **parent process** is killed then always the child process is also terminated.

                                                                              Yes (   ) No (   )

544. The **shell** in UNIX starts immediately as soon as power is on.   Yes (   ) No (   )

545. The value of v after execution of v=`expr 2 + 5 ` is 5.   Yes (   ) No (   )

546. Major device numbers and minor device numbers are associated with special files

                                                                              Yes (   ) No (   )

547. **UNIX shell** is also a programming language.   Yes (   ) No (   )

548. **vi** is a screen editor.   Yes (   ) No (   )

549. It is possible to execute all **ed** commands under vi using ":"   Yes (   ) No (   )

550. The **test** command can be applied over strings and files but not on numeric values.

                                                                              Yes (   ) No (   )

551. The parameters of awk command can also be fed through a file. **Yes** ( ) **No** ( )

552. After core dump error a running program will be terminated. **Yes** ( ) **No** ( )

553. The UNIX system call **signal** is used to handle interrupts. **Yes** ( ) **No** ( )

554. **System calls** are only used by operating system. **Yes** ( ) **No** ( )

555. **set** command is used to make a variable global in C shell. **Yes** ( ) **No** ( )

556. **Create system call** fails even if there are already many files are opened.

   Yes ( ) **No** ( )

557. **cc -d "pop = 0"** **Yes** ( ) **No** ( )

   In the above command -D "pop-0" is equivalent to preprocessor directive the c code ,
   ie #include pop 0.

558. **tr** is the non-interactive stream editor. **Yes** ( ) **No** ( )

559. Through **C language programs** a user can access **OS functions**. **Yes** ( ) **No** ( )

560. In UNIX, **process management** is hierarchical. **Yes** ( ) **No** ( )

561. **sys_errlist** is a UNIX systems global variable which maintains the diagnostic
   messages corresponding to system call error numbers that are listed in the system.

   Yes ( ) **No** ( )

562. In concurrent programming, **process** and **task** are same. **Yes** ( ) **No** ( )

563. **u pointer** is maintained by kernel which keeps the address of the currently running
   process. **Yes** ( ) **No** ( )

564. **exec()** system internally calls execve() system call. **Yes** ( ) **No** ( )

565. The **kernel encapsulates** the hardware and provides UNIX system services to
   application programs. **Yes** ( ) **No** ( )

566. **Process can not modify their environments directly,** rather they can request
   modifications through system calls to the OS. **Yes** ( ) **No** ( )

567. **vfork** and **fork** are same. **Yes** ( ) **No** ( )

568. **traps** are caused by program exceptions such as references to bad addresses or
   attempts to execute undefined operation codes. **Yes** ( ) **No** ( )

569. **setuid** bit of a file can be set by only owner of the file or super user.

   Yes ( ) **No** ( )

570. Always **effective UID and real UID** are same. **Yes** ( ) **No** ( )

571. If a programs **setuid bit is on** then any user can execute that program.

   Yes ( ) **No** ( )

572. If **root makes setuid bit off to passwd command** (executable) file then users can run
   passwd command to change their password. **Yes** ( ) **No** ( )

573. **UNIX system delay physical writes** until a buffer is needed. **Yes** ( ) **No** ( )

574. **Signals are software mechanisms** similar to hardware interrupts. **Yes** ( ) **No** ( )

575. **Signals** are used for inter process communication. **Yes** ( ) **No** ( )

576. **sbrk** call uses a memory size increment or decrement. **Yes** ( ) **No** ( )

577. **malloc** uses **brk** system call.   **Yes ( ) No ( )**
578. The **open** call creates descriptors for files and devices.   **Yes ( ) No ( )**
579. **trap** command is not available in C shell?.   **Yes ( ) No ( )**
580. **chsh** command asks your password while running.   **Yes ( ) No ( )**
581. **!5:3** at command line gets third word in 5'th command in history buffer.

                                                                                   Yes ( ) No ( )
582. **/etc/shadow** contains same information as that of /etc/passwd.   **Yes ( ) No ( )**
583. In **/etc/passwd** file second field contains encrypted password.   **Yes ( ) No ( )**
584. In **/etc/passwd** file second field is actually key for encryption.   **Yes ( ) No ( )**
585. When you enter password at login prompt encryption takes place. **Yes ( ) No ( )**
586. **Password can be given to group** also.   **Yes ( ) No ( )**
587. If you **enter wrong username** still login process gives passwd prompt.

                                                                                   Yes ( ) No ( )
588. **uptime** displays details of time, number of users working, from how many days they
     are running, load etc.   **Yes ( ) No ( )**
589. C shell supports **++** to variables.   **Yes ( ) No ( )**
590. **chsh** command is used to change your default shell.   **Yes ( ) No ( )**
591. Is there any **POSIX** shell?.   **Yes ( ) No ( )**
592. Does the following command works similarly?.
     cat < xyz >pqr 2>&1
     cat < xyz 2>&1 >pqr   **Yes ( ) No ( )**
593. Unlike **Bourne shell, C shell** maintains an internal **hash table** for finding commands.

                                                                                   Yes ( ) No ( )
594. **rehash** equivalent command in Bourne shell is upate.   **Yes ( ) No ( )**
595. **C shell** does not support a separate redirection for standard error. **Yes ( ) No ( )**
596. Is this is a valid bourn shell command sequence?.   **Yes ( ) No ( )**
     @a=2
     @b=3
     @c = $a + $b
     echo $a $b $c

597. **perl** is interpreted scripting language.   **Yes ( ) No ( )**
598. In **perl** variables should not be **declared explicitly**.   **Yes ( ) No ( )**
599. In both **awk** and **perl** variables default values is zero.   **Yes ( ) No ( )**
600. In **perl**, arrays and **associative arrays** (hashes) are available.   **Yes ( ) No ( )**
601. Both **awk** and **perl** produce **associative arrays**.   **Yes ( ) No ( )**
602. **File handler** are special variable in perl.   **Yes ( ) No ( )**
603. **C** and **C++** supports associative arrays.   **Yes ( ) No ( )**

604. **cc** command available in 1989 which is proposed by **ISO.C** is available in POSIX specification of UNIX. **Yes ( ) No ( )**

605. All the variables are defined at the top of a block in C language thus while compiling **symbol table** generation becomes easy. **Yes ( ) No ( )**

606. **Java** and **S-Algol** are interpreted languages. **Yes ( ) No ( )**

607. **-S** option in **SunOS** with **cc** compiler will create **assembly program** of given C program. **Yes ( ) No ( )**

608. **Inline** takes assembly codes and puts them together in a single assembly-language program. **Yes ( ) No ( )**

609. **strip** command removes symbol table from an executable file. **Yes ( ) No ( )**

610. **/etc/inittab** file fields are separated by #. **Yes ( ) No ( )**

611. **Loop-back** interface in Ethernet can be used to see whether one can communicate with local Ethernet or not. **Yes ( ) No ( )**

612. On **WAN** every machine is available for administrator. **Yes ( ) No ( )**

613. Is it possible to **check files** in filesystem based on **last modified time**. **Yes ( ) No ( )**

614. **Ethernet and IP addresses** are same. **Yes ( ) No ( )**

615. Is it possible to have **multiple IP numbers** to a machine?. **Yes ( ) No ( )**

616. **UDP** is faster than **TCP** but less reliable. **Yes ( ) No ( )**

617. **UDP** is **stated** protocol whereas **TCP** is **stateless** protocol. **Yes ( ) No ( )**

618. **Presentation layer** converts the data into machine dependent form. **Yes ( ) No ( )**

619. **Port mapper** duty is to connect two daemons. **Yes ( ) No ( )**

620. Is there any difference in the outputs of the following commands?. **Yes ( ) No ( )**
    (a) **ls -Rfl** (b) **find . -print**

621. **ls a[^c][^b]** pattern matches abc?. **Yes ( ) No ( )**

622. `umask` only removes bits from default mask, it never sets bits which were not already set in default mask. **Yes ( ) No ( )**

623. As **t-bit** is set for directories like the mail spool area and /tmp they are writable to everyone, but should not allow a user to delete another user's files. **Yes ( ) No ( )**

624. Usually **stderr** will arrive before to stdout. **Yes ( ) No ( )**

625. **script** command is same is history. **Yes ( ) No ( )**

626. Does the single quotes prevent *variable substitution* and *sub-shells?*. **Yes ( ) No ( )**

627. C shell does not allow **subroutines or functions**. **Yes ( ) No ( )**

628. **Job number and PID** are same. **Yes ( ) No ( )**

629. **Job numbers** are assigned by kernel. **Yes ( ) No ( )**

630.　In C shell one can create a **local shell**, with its own private variables by enclosing commands in parentheses.　　　　　　　　　　**Yes (　) No (　)**

631.　In Bourne shell = ~ can not be used with if condition.　　**Yes (　) No (　)**

632.　There is no real facility for **arrays in the Bourne shell**.　　**Yes (　) No (　)**

633.　One way in which functions differ from **external scripts** is that the shell does not spawn a sub shell to execute them.　　　　　　　**Yes (　) No (　)**

634.　To deny all access to group and others, the command **umask 077** can be used.　　　　　　　　　　　　　　　　　　　**Yes (　) No (　)**

635.　If x1 and x2 are two commands which are having standard output then **(x1;x2)|x3** command can be used to pipe output of x1 and x2 to command x3. **Yes (　) No (　)**

636.　For non-login interactive shells, if ~/.bashrc exists, it will be sourced.

　　　　　　　　　　　　　　　　　　　　　　　　　Yes (　) No (　)

637.　The following two aliases are defined. While executing the second alias command does the **rm** is taken as **rm -i**?.　　　　　　**Yes (　) No (　)**

　　alias rm='rm -i'

　　alias rmtrash='rm /tmp/*.tmp'

638.　Does the alias commands are inheritable, i.e alias commands defined in the parent shell are available in sub-shells?.　　　　　　　**Yes (　) No (　)**

639.　Does the alias commands defined in sub shells are available in the parent shell, i.e even after the expiry of child shell?.　　　　　　**Yes (　) No (　)**

640.　Does the following command works?.　　　　　　　　**Yes (　) No (　)**
　　cmd 2>&1 > out.txt &

641.　**biff** command is asynchronous mail notification command.　**Yes (　) No (　)**

642.　**clri** command can be executed by super-user only?.　　**Yes (　) No (　)**

643.　The following function (xcd) can be used to change prompt in Bourne shell.

　　xcd() { cd $* ; PS1="`pwd` $ "; }　　　　　　　**Yes (　) No (　)**

644.　In tcsh **%c or %.** the trailing component of the current directory.

　　　　　　　　　　　　　　　　　　　　　　　　　Yes (　) No (　)

645.　Does the following work in Bourne shell?.
　　while (1)　　　　　　　　　　　　　　　　　**Yes (　) No (　)**
　　**　set line = "$<"**
　　**　if ("$line" == "") break**
　　end

646.　Does the following shell script in korn shell changes filenames upper to lower.
　　typeset -l l
　　for f in *;
　　**　do**
　　**　l="$f"**
　　**　mv $f $l**
　　done

647. OS hides the truth about HW from programmer and presents the simple oriented interface to do I/O operations. **Yes** ( ) **No** ( )

648. The devices in UNIX system do not have index numbers. **Yes** ( ) **No** ( )

649. A file system consists of two things - the data file and the i-node. **Yes** ( ) **No** ( )

650. Many UNIX commands use built in shell variables. **Yes** ( ) **No** ( )

651. More is a filer. **Yes** ( ) **No** ( )

652. awk command can take decisions. **Yes** ( ) **No** ( )

653. In UNIX one file system can span multiple physical disks. **Yes** ( ) **No** ( )

654. "fork" system call is the only way for process to create process. **Yes** ( ) **No** ( )

655. **X windows** is a server. **Yes** ( ) **No** ( )

656. **uucp** is a batch processing/spooling system. **Yes** ( ) **No** ( )

657. To function **uucp** mail, sh and cron are required. **Yes** ( ) **No** ( )

658. Caching is also done by **resolver** to further reduce load on name server.
Yes ( ) **No** ( )

659. One of the **TCP connection** created by **rsh** is used for both Standard input and standard output. **Yes** ( ) **No** ( )

660. While **FTPing username** can not be root. **Yes** ( ) **No** ( )

661. **vnode** and **inode** are same. **Yes** ( ) **No** ( )

662. **/etc/ethers** file contains Ethernet addresses. **Yes** ( ) **No** ( )

663. **/etc/mtab** and /etc/xtab contains same information. **Yes** ( ) **No** ( )

664. **export** command can be used to make file systems to be available to remote machines. **Yes** ( ) **No** ( )

665. **/usr/etc/biod** is used to improve NFS performance. **Yes** ( ) **No** ( )

666. **biod demon**'s allow a client to make read-ahead and write-behind requests to a remote file system. **Yes** ( ) **No** ( )

667. Shell does not start a separate process to run an internal command. **Yes** ( ) **No** ( )

668. The search path is built-into the shell. **Yes** ( ) **No** ( )

669. UNIX will be in single user mode when one user is working especially on PC based UNIX systems such as Linux. **Yes** ( ) **No** ( )

670. UNIX does not have any concept of file version like VAX/VMS. **Yes** ( ) **No** ( )

671. In UNIX, wildcard * matches period(.) also. **Yes** ( ) **No** ( )

672. Maximum number of files a file system can hold can be easily adjusted at any stage.

673. Is it possible to happen a file system to run out of i-nodes and give file can not be created error message?. **Yes** ( ) **No** ( )

674. When a file whose SGID, SUID are copied, do they retain their properties?.
Yes ( ) **No** ( )

675. When you are editing through vi, CTRL Z will take you to shell. **Yes** ( ) **No** ( )

676. In UNIX, **linefeed** is end of line marker and in DOS carriage return and linefeed serves the same functionality. Yes ( ) No ( )

677. When a sub shell (Bourne) is started **.profile** file will not be executed.

Yes ( ) No ( )

678. Does the sub shell (Korn) uses the **configuration file** pointed by **ENV** environment variable?. Yes ( ) No ( )

679. Both login Korn shell and Bourne shells use **.profile** file. Yes ( ) No ( )

680. **Kernel** interacts with processes and devices. Yes ( ) No ( )

681. The **Intel 80x86** provides four rings of execution levels. Yes ( ) No ( )

682. There is only one instance of **Kernel** running in the system irrespective of how many processes are running. Yes ( ) No ( )

683. **Context switching** and **mode switching** are same. Yes ( ) No ( )

684. Each process contains its **Kernel stack** in its address space. Yes ( ) No ( )

685. While **Kernel is in system context**, global operations such as interrupt handling will be still continuing. Yes ( ) No ( )

686. **Swapper** and **pagedaemon** are initiated by **init** process. Yes ( ) No ( )

687. **Exceptions** are synchronous to the process and are caused by events related to process itself. Yes ( ) No ( )

688. Both **SW** and **HW** interrupts are handled in process context. Yes ( ) No ( )

689. When an **interrupt (HW) is occurred** then the current process will not enjoy its current time slice completely because of interrupt service time. Yes ( ) No ( )

690. **UNIX system preempts** low-priority interrupt to carry high priority interrupts.

Yes ( ) No ( )

691. If **a process is running in Kernel mode** it can not be preempted by other processes even if the first one's time slice is over. Yes ( ) No ( )

692. A Process goes to **Zombie state** if it dies before its parent and parent does not call **wait()**. Yes ( ) No ( )

693. When a process is not running then **process table** is not accessible to Kernel.

Yes ( ) No ( )

694. **Vnodes** means virtual nodes which belongs to process management.

Yes ( ) No ( )

695. **vfork()** is faster than **fork()** Yes ( ) No ( )

696. **vfork()** copies parents address map to child as soon as it is called. Yes ( ) No ( )

697. **Several disks** may be combined into a single logical disk or volume.

Yes ( ) No ( )

698. Creating **hard links** to directories is **barred** for users except for super user.

                                                            Yes ( ) No ( )

699. Pathnames in **symbolic links** are always absolute.   **Yes ( ) No ( )**

700. Random number function rand() is part of UNIX math library.   **Yes ( ) No ( )**

701. Physical files are stored as blocks.   **Yes ( ) No ( )**

Answers for Multiple Choice Questions

1.	B	31.	B	61.	B	91.	C
2.	B	32.	B	62.	C	92.	B
3.	A	33.	C	63.	C	93.	B
4.	B	34.	B	64.	A	94.	A
5.	A	35.	B	65.	B	95.	C
6.	D	36.	D	66.	B	96.	D
7.	D	37.	A	67.	B	97.	C
8.	A	38.	B	68.	A	98.	C
9.	A	39.	A	69.	E	99.	A
10.	D	40.	D	70.	A	100.	E
11.	B	41.	D	71.	D	101.	C
12.	B	42.	D	72.	B	102.	B
13.	A	43.	A	73.	B	103.	B
14.	A	44.	C	74.	B	104.	B
15.	A	45.	C	75.	C	105.	B
16.	A	46.	A	76.	C	106.	C
17.	C	47.	C	77.	A	107.	A
18.	D	48.	A	78.	D	108.	C
19.	C	49.	A	79.	C	109.	D
20.	B	50.	C	80.	B	110.	C
21.	C	51.	A	81.	D	111.	C
22.	D	52.	B	82.	C	112.	A
23.	C	53.	B	83.	A	113.	C
24.	A	54.	C	84.	D	114.	C
25.	C	55.	B	85.	B	115.	D
26.	C	56.	A	86.	C	116.	C
27.	C	57.	C	87.	B	117.	B
28.	C	58.	C	88.	D	118.	C
29.	C	59.	D	89.	C	119.	B
30.	C	60.	C	90.	C	120.	C

121.	B	157.	A	193.	D	229.	A
122.	A	158.	C	194.	B	230.	A
123.	C	159.	D	195.	D	231.	B
124.	C	160.	D	196.	C	232.	D
125.	B	161.	D	197.	A	233.	D
126.	C	162.	B	198.	C	234.	C
127.	D	163.	C	199.	C	235.	D
128.	C	164.	B	200.	D	236.	A
129.	B	165.	D	201.	A	237.	C
130.	C	166.	C	202.	B	238.	A
131.	B	167.	B	203.	C	239.	B
132.	C	168.	D	204.	B	240.	C
133.	B	169.	B	205.	B	241.	B
134.	C	170.	B	206.	A	242.	B
135.	C	171.	A	207.	B	243.	A
136.	C	172.	C	208.	C	244.	C
137.	C	173.	C	209.	A	245.	D
138.	C	174.	C	210.	A	246.	A
139.	B	175.	A	211.	A	247.	C
140.	B	176.	D	212.	B	248.	B
141.	D(XT)	177.	C	213.	A	249.	B
142.	B	178.	C	214.	A	250.	A
143.	C	179.	A	215.	C	251.	C
144.	C	180.	D	216.	C	252.	C
145.	C	181.	C	217.	C	253.	E
146.	C	182.	B	218.	C	254.	C
147.	A	183.	E	219.	B	255.	A
148.	D	184.	A	220.	C	256.	C
149.	C	185.	C	221.	C	257.	B
150.	B	186.	C	222.	D	258.	A
151.	B	187.	C	223.	C	259.	B
152.	A	188.	D	224.	A	260.	C
153.	A	189.	C	225.	B	261.	C
154.	C	190.	C	226.	C	262.	B
155.	D	191.	D	227.	C	263.	B
156.	D	192.	C	228.	D	264.	A

265.	B	301.	A	337.	B	373.	C
266.	C	302.	C	338.	D	374.	D
267.	C	303.	D	339.	D	375.	C
268.	B	304.	A	340.	A	376.	C
269.	B	305.	C	341.	A	377.	D
270.	B	306.	B	342.	B	378.	C
271.	C	307.	A	343.	D	379.	A
272.	A	308.	B	344.	A	380.	A
273.	B	309.	D	345.	D	381.	D
274.	A	310.	D	346.	C	382.	C
275.	A	311.	D	347.	A	383.	D
276.	A	312.	D	348.	D	384.	C
277.	D	313.	C	349.	D	385.	D
278.	A	314.	D	350.	D	386.	D
279.	B	315.	D	351.	B	387.	C
280.	B	316.	D	352.	B	388.	A
281.	C	317.	C	353.	C	389.	D
282.	C	318.	C	354.	C	390.	C
283.	D	319.	A	355.	D	391.	C
284.	A	320.	C	356.	A	392.	C
285.	C	321.	A	357.	C	393.	D
286.	C	322.	A	358.	B	394.	A
287.	D	323.	A	359.	B	395.	C
288.	A	324.	B	360.	A	396.	C
289.	C	325.	B	361.	B	397.	C
290.	D	326.	D	362.	A	398.	C
291.	A	327.	C	363.	A	399.	D
292.	D	328.	B	364.	A	400.	C
293.	D	329.	D	365.	B	401.	D
294.	B	330.	B	366.	B	402.	C
295.	D	331.	D	367.	B	403.	B
296.	C	332.	E	368.	B	404.	A
297.	C	333.	D	369.	A	405.	D
298.	D	334.	D	370.	B	406.	D
299.	A	335.	A	371.	A	407.	C
300.	B	336.	D	372.	C	408.	B

409.	D	418.	C	427.	D	436.	C
410.	D	419.	D	428.	B	437.	D
411.	D	420.	B	429.	C	438.	B
412.	D	421.	A	430.	D	439.	B
413.	C	422.	A	431.	C	440.	C
414.	D	423.	D	432.	A	441.	C
415.	C	424.	B	433.	C	442.	C
416.	C	425.	D	434.	A		
417.	D	426.	A	435.	A		

Answers to Fill in the Blanks

1. korn
2. unprintable characters also in filenames.
3. ?
4. awk
5. Bourne & C
6. none
7. ;;
8. command
9. higher
10. /etc/passwd
11. three (standard input, output, and error)
12. 01
13. rm –r
14. cat
15. read and write
16. stderr
17. keyboard
18. pipe
19. alphabet
20. IFS
21. PS1
22. export
23. login
24. $0
25. command (shell script name)
26. $?
27. expr
28. ;
29. shell script
30. command2||command1
31. filenames in PWD in four columns
32. #
33. ;
34. zero
35. the number of bytes
36. cut
37. fork
38. buffer
39. i-node
40. non-printable
41. other than zero
42. vi –r xyz
43. lpstat –d
44. ls –F
45. are not
46. sccs
47. files in previous working directory
48. path of present working directory
49. shell
50. real
51. getpid()
52. mount
53. talk
54. PS2
55. Ken Thompson
56. ps
57. *
58. who
59. $?
60. lex
61. nice
62. touch

63. yacc
64. displays how many users using a specified shell in a tabular fashion
65. shell names which are used by users
66. PWD and /usr/include
67. where to look for include files.
68. libc, I/O and memory manipulation functions
69. names of the shells which are used by one user only
70. Guess
71. When a program is under execution, kernel will be in user mode and when you call system call, it will be going to kernel mode after which system returns to normal user mode.
72. the way how they communicate and deliver the messages.
73. system call
74. piping
75. Environment
76. sed
77. kernel
78. supervisor call
79. i-node
80. screen
81. grep
82. export
83. test
84. -d or -f with if statement
85. zero
86. dependent
87. system(x)
88. /etc/passwd
89. banner
90. PS1
91. /etc/profile
92. wall
93. fsck
94. data block of the directory in which the file presents
95. linked list
96. what lines to be added to
97. number of lines, characters, and words
98. last 10 lines
99. user details in sorted order who are
100. system configurations
101. &, background
102. any single character, *
103. p1 is failed
104. 111, a+x
105. a program crashes
106. filenames with extension back under /aab directory.
107. files of users in /home and accessed 3 days before.
108. c and pascal programs under /home directory.
109. copy input/output
110. copies files to magnetic tape which are newer than the last log file.
111. ioctl
112. super
113. calling process
114. **grep "^string$" abc**
115. other than lower case a-z.
116. export
117. super user
118. write
119. paste
120. kernel
121. doscp or dos2unix or todos
122. inherited
123. signal
124. mv
125. finger
126. shell
127. process

128. 14 (now it is relaxed)

129. Hierarchical

130. daemon

131. Ken Thompson

132. filters

133. /etc/inittab

134. /dev/null

135. touch

136. diff

137. cmp

138. Guess

139. nohup

140. number of records read till that point.

141. no of empty lines in the file specified in filename.

142. **ls -l $* |awk '{print $5 "\t" $9 }' -**

143. simultaneous peripheral output on-line

144. makefile or Makefile

145. create new device file

146. searches a library archive for function dependencies and prints.

147. striping out unnecessary stuff from executable files otherwise which is needed for debugging etc.

148. binds multiple object-code files into a single executable file.

149. only details of directories in P.W.D.

150. link details of files in a column

151. no. of files

152. same

153. not same

154. CTRL+Z and bg

155. 2 bytes

156. files not owned by any user specified in /etc/passwd file.

157. names of the files which are

158. bad blocks

159. 5

160. update

161. –r

162. device busy

163. can not

164. *

165. kept in .profile

166. then you can not delete or rename files in it

167. sticky bit to directory

168. root

169. **grep "[0-9]$" filename.**

170. CTRL + D

171. Standard input, standard output and standard error.

172. a pointer a structure.

173. chmod +t

174. 32767

175. faster, slower

176. 0,0

177. Data Encryption Standards

178. which does not start with a vowel

179. major and minor device numbers

180. 4 and 65 respectively

181. buffered, un-buffered

182. 48 K

183. block size

184. bootstrap loader

185. free space in blocks

186. touch

187. ls –lu

188. ASCII

189. output only unique lines   last access time of a file.

190. information between columns 1 to 5 of each line of the specified file.

191. Tab space

192. inquire the status of **uucp jobs.**

193. **DEAD** environment variable

194. msgget
195. substitute last argument of previous command i.e. a1.c.
196. to change time stamp of a file to present time.
197. not same
198. stdin, stdout, stderr
199. return
200. display last screen
201. cannot
202. login times and usernames sorted alphabetically.
203. external, errno
204. maximum
205. its argument does not point to a currently open channel.
206. relates a program name to set of words.
207. executes ls -t | sort
208. login directory of current user
209. null
210. system calls, disk I/O operations, efficiency.
211. utmp
212. isxdigit
213. duplicates an opened files descriptor and returns the new file descriptor.
214. 32MB
215. you
216. if file sizes are very small.
217. .login
218. all environment variables information.
219. forget environment variables.
220. primary prompt string value
221. stores number of shell command lines to save when you logout.
222. C
223. clears four times directory stack.
224. a process (invisible to users) that extends important system services.
225. FIFO
226. some irreconcilable inconsistency is detected in its internal data structure.
227. POSIX
228. a program that reads the kernel image at boot time into RAM.
229. long integer
230. process table
231. xxx variable is defined
232. change destination of standard error file.
233. both standard error and standard output
234. |&
235. directory stack
236. filenames in the P.W.D starts with e and with no separate spaces.
237. to change working environment in C shell, home directory of the user.
238. make a background process to run even after you logout.
239. hang-up
240. 3 lines with hello.
241. first *, all file names of P.W.D, and file names of 3 characters length.
242. root
243. directory
244. :. o.
245. Guess
246. export in bourn and setenv in C shell.
247. BEGIN{actions}
248. segment violation or memory fault.
249. present directory
250. fork
251. su
252. nohup
253. sync
254. excessive movement of page back & forth between memory and disk
255. lprm

256. foreach

257. cd

258. None

259. list of shell variables which are defined as readonly.

260. A list of name/value pairs that are passed to each child process from its parent process.

261. 10 -b 70 -c 81 and 5 in two subsequent lines.

262. save the path of the present directory.

263. number of commands C shell can

264. filenames of P.W.D followed by the above command string.

265. /user/bin /bin /tmp

266. PS1="hello".

267. name of the command line interpreter (CLI) to be applied for that file.

268. deletes all files mno in all the directories whose names starts with mno

269. shared memory approach

270. can not have

271. pipes, messages, semaphores, and sockets.

272. special files

273. descriptors

274. major and minor numbers

275. descriptors for the read and write ends

276. Microsoft

277. super

278. periodically writes all the unwritten buffered to disk.

279. sub

280. daemon

281. #

282. passwd, login

283. group string, password, GID, and usernames separated by comma.

284. uucp

285. Bourne again shell

286. alias

287. C

288. bad command. Command not found.

289. back quotes

290. C

291. chsh

292. !?word

293. Guess

294. practical extensible report language

295. program is given along command line.

296. both single and double quotes.

297. evaluates

298. zzzmmm (no space between).

299. array indexes are strings.

300. file handle

301. preprocessor

302. program text, data, relocation information, a symbol table, string table.

303. structure of executable file with size of its components such as   text area, data area, etc.

304. contain listing of all strings used in the program.

305. strip

306. compiles hello.c program.

307. -ll

308. MAC

309. 24

310. 127

311. 25

312. /etc/inetd.conf

313. external data representation.

314. 111
315. display filenames in multi-column fashion in each line file lines will be sorted.
316. find
317. files whose sizes are greater than 1 MB
318. files whose sizes are smaller than 1MB.
319. to change default shell
320. a network attack
321. apropos
322. A protocol compiler which generates C code from a higher level language, for programming RPC applications.
323. associated
324. cd: shell built-in command
325. external command
326. which changes the file extension of all files ending in `.x' to the same name with a `.y' extension. This cannot work in UNIX, because the shell tries expands everything before passing the arguments to the command line.
327. the first one displays those lines which starts with '#' and the other displays those lines which does not start with '#'.
328. egrep '(^[^A-Z])'   filename
329. egrep '([^#][\!*\&])' filename
330. Since the shell has the interpret them by reading
331. it should be executed with the permissions and rights of owner of the file.
332. Whether the file is regular plain file or directory etc.
333. restrict the deletion
334. owner or the super user
335. C

336. when a variable is defined irrespective of whether it has a value or not.
337. =
338. a b c d
339. set noclobber
340. appends stdout, stderr to file pqr ignoring noclobber.
341. either single or double quotes
342. **kill -19 333**
343. C
344. 2
345. C
346. inside parenthesis
347. raju.c
348. changes the default so that all variables, after the command are created *global*
349. (No analogy)
350. not external; through expr command.
351. executable and linking format used recently in place of a.out format
352. basename $x
353. lost+found
354. set prompt='%~ '
355. are not
356. awk & perl
357. .login file in Bourne shell
358. nu
359. boot program
360. /etc/motd
361. i-node
362. fg
363. %f
364. the one in which each network request is satisfied without reference to previous request.
365. uucp
366. UNIX-to-UNIX copy in copy out
367. 256

368. two
369. file handle
370. linefeed whose ASCII code is 012
371. internal command
372. number of i-nodes that are created when file system is created.
373. fg
374. .profile
375. 10ms
376. loading Kernel from disk
377. kernel
378. protection
379. when a process makes a system call, it executes a set of instructions to goto Kernel mode which is known as mode switch.
380. bootstrapping
381. 1
382. traps
383. despatch table
384. nice value and usage factor
385. During fork() call execution parents pages are marked as copy-on-write such that if child wants to change a page, page fault will occur and that pages copy is loaded which is writable by the child. By doing this when a child expires same pages which are marked are used by parent without loading them again.
386. the address of the first instruction that the program must execute.
387. 32
388. param.h
389. query name servers on behalf of clients

Answers for True or False

1.	N	25.	Y	49.	Y	73.	Y
2.	Y	26.	Y	50.	Y	74.	N
3.	N	27.	Y	51.	N	75.	N
4.	N	28.	Y	52.	N	76.	Y
5.	Y	29.	Y	53.	Y	77.	Y
6.	N	30.	Y	54.	N	78.	Y
7.	N	31.	N	55.	Y	79.	N
8.	N	32.	Y	56.	Y	80.	Y
9.	Y	33.	Y	57.	N	81.	N
10.	Y	34.	N	58.	Y	82.	Y
11.	Y	35.	Y	59.	Y	83.	N
12.	Y	36.	N	60.	N	84.	Y
13.	N	37.	Y	61.	Y	85.	Y
14.	N	38.	N	62.	N	86.	Y
15.	Y	39.	Y	63.	Y	87.	N
16.	N	40.	Y	64.	Y	88.	N
17.	Y	41.	Y	65.	Y	89.	Y
18.	Y	42.	Y	66.	N	90.	Y
19.	N	43.	Y	67.	Y	91.	N
20.	Y	44.	Y	68.	N	92.	Y
21.	Y	45.	Y	69.	N	93.	Y
22.	Y	46.	Y	70.	Y	94.	Y
23.	Y	47.	N	71.	Y	95.	Y
24.	N	48.	Y	72.	N	96.	Y

No.	Ans	No.	Ans	No.	Ans	No.	Ans
97.	Y	126.	Y	155.	Y	184.	Y
98.	Y	127.	Y	156.	N	185.	Y
99.	Y	128.	Y	157.	Y	186.	Y
100.	N	129.	N	158.	Y	187.	Y
101.	Y	130.	Y	159.	N	188.	Y
102.	Y	131.	Y	160.	Y	189.	Y
103.	N	132.	Y	161.	Y	190.	N
104.	N	133.	N	162.	N	191.	Y
105.	Y	134.	N	163.	Y	192.	N
106.	Y	135.	N	164.	N	193.	N
107.	Y	136.	Y	165.	Y	194.	Y
108.	Y	137.	N	166.	Y	195.	Y
109.	Y	138.	Y	167.	N	196.	Y
110.	Y	139.	Y	168.	N	197.	Answer
111.	N	140.	N	169.	N	198.	N
112.	N	141.	N	170.	Y	199.	Y
113.	N	142.	Y	171.	N	200.	Y
114.	Y	143.	Y	172.	Y	201.	Y
115.	N	144.	Y	173.	N	202.	Y
116.	Y	145.	N	174.	N	203.	N
117.	Y	146.	N	175.	N	204.	Y
118.	N	147.	Y	176.	Y	205.	N
119.	N	148.	N	177.	Y	206.	N
120.	Y	149.	Y	178.	Y	207.	N
121.	Y	150.	Y	179.	N	208.	Y
122.	Y	151.	Y	180.	N	209.	Y
123.	N	152.	Answer	181.	N	210.	Y
124.	N	153.	Y	182.	Y	211.	Y
125.	Y	154.	Y	183.	Y	212.	Y

No.	Ans	No.	Ans	No.	Ans	No.	Ans
213.	Y	242.	Y	271.	Y	300.	N
214.	Y	243.	Answer	272.	N	301.	N
215.	Y	244.	N	273.	Y	302.	Y
216.	Y	245.	N	274.	N	303.	N
217.	Y	246.	N	275.	Y	304.	Y
218.	N	247.	N	276.	N	305.	Y
219.	Y	248.	Y	277.	N	306.	N
220.	Y	249.	N	278.	Y	307.	N
221.	Y	250.	N	279.	Y	308.	Y
222.	N	251.	Y	280.	N	309.	N
223.	Y	252.	Y	281.	N	310.	N
224.	Y	253.	Y	282.	N	311.	Y
225.	N	254.	N	283.	N	312.	N
226.	Y	255.	Y	284.	Y	313.	N
227.	N	256.	Y	285.	Y	314.	N
228.	Y	257.	N	286.	Y	315.	Y
229.	Y	258.	Y	287.	Y	316.	N
230.	Y	259.	N	288.	Y	317.	Y
231.	Y	260.	Y	289.	Y	318.	Y
232.	Y	261.	Y	290.	Y	319.	N
233.	Y	262.	Y	291.	Y	320.	Answer
234.	Y	263.	N	292.	Y	321.	Y
235.	Y	264.	N	293.	N	322.	Answer
236.	N	265.	Y	294.	Y	323.	Y
237.	N	266.	Y	295.	Y	324.	Y
238.	N	267.	Y	296.	Y	325.	N
239.	N	268.	N	297.	Y	326.	Y
240.	N	269.	Y	298.	Y	327.	Y
241.	N	270.	N	299.	N	328.	Y

329.	Y	358.	N	387.	Y	416.	N
330.	Y	359.	Y	388.	Answer	417.	N
331.	Y	360.	Y	389.	Y	418.	N
332.	Y	361.	Y	390.	Y	419.	N
333.	N	362.	Y	391.	Answer	420.	Y
334.	Answer	363.	Y	392.	Answer	421.	Y
335.	Answer	364.	Y	393.	Answer	422.	N
336.	Y	365.	N	394.	Answer	423.	N
337.	Y	366.	Y	395.	Answer	424.	Y
338.	Y	367.	Answer	396.	Y	425.	Y
339.	Y	368.	Y	397.	Y	426.	Y
340.	Y	369.	Y	398.	Answer	427.	N
341.	Y	370.	Y	399.	Y	428.	Answer
342.	Y	371.	N	400.	Y	429.	Answer
343.	Y	372.	N	401.	N	430.	Y
344.	Y	373.	N	402.	N	431.	Answer
345.	Y	374.	N	403.	Y	432.	N
346.	Y	375.	Y	404.	Y	433.	Y
347.	N	376.	Y	405.	Y	434.	Y
348.	N	377.	N	406.	Y	435.	Y
349.	Y	378.	N	407.	Y	436.	N
350.	N	379.	Y	408.	Y	437.	N
351.	Y	380.	Y	409.	Y	438.	Y
352.	Y	381.	N	410.	N	439.	N
353.	N	382.	Y	411.	Y	440.	Y
354.	Y	383.	Y	412.	N	441.	N
355.	Y	384.	N	413.	Y	442.	Y
356.	N	385.	Y	414.	Y	443.	Y
357.	Y	386.	Y	415.	Y	444.	Y

445.	Answer	474.	N	503.	N	532.	Y
446.	Y	475.	Y	504.	N	533.	Y
447.	N	476.	N	505.	Y	534.	Y
448.	Y	477.	Y	506.	Y	535.	N
449.	Y	478.	Y	507.	N	536.	Y
450.	Y	479.	Y	508.	Y	537.	N
451.	N	480.	N	509.	N	538.	Y
452.	Y	481.	N	510.	Y	539.	N
453.	N	482.	N	511.	N	540.	N
454.	N	483.	Answer	512.	N	541.	Y
455.	Y	484.	N	513.	Y	542.	Y
456.	N	485.	N	514.	N	543.	N
457.	N	486.	Y	515.	Y	544.	N
458.	Y	487.	Y	516.	N	545.	N
459.	N	488.	N	517.	N	546.	Y
460.	N	489.	N	518.	Y	547.	N
461.	N	490.	Y	519.	N	548.	Y
462.	N	491.	Y	520.	N	549.	Answer
463.	N	492.	N	521.	N	550.	N
464.	Y	493.	N	522.	N	551.	Answer
465.	N	494.	Y	523.	Y	552.	Y
466.	Y	495.	N	524.	N	553.	Y
467.	N	496.	Y	525.	Y	554.	N
468.	Y	497.	N	526.	N	555.	N
469.	N	498.	Y	527.	N	556.	Y
470.	N	499.	N	528.	Y	557.	Answer
471.	Y	500.	Y	529.	N	558.	Y
472.	Y	501.	Y	530.	N	559.	Y
473.	Y	502.	N	531.	N	560.	Y

561.	Y	590.	Y	619.	Y	648.	Y
562.	N	591.	Y	620.	Y	649.	N
563.	Y	592.	N	621.	N	650.	N
564.	Y	593.	Y	622.	Y	651.	N
565.	Y	594.	N	623.	Y	652.	Y
566.	Y	595.	Y	624.	Y	653.	N
567.	N	596.	N	625.	N	654.	Y
568.	Y	597.	Y	626.	Y	655.	Y
569.	Y	598.	Y	627.	Y	656.	Y
570.	N	599.	Y	628.	N	657.	Y
571.	Answer	600.	Y	629.	N	658.	Y
572.	N	601.	N	630.	Y	659.	Y
573.	Y	602.	Y	631.	Y	660.	Y
574.	Y	603.	N	632.	Y	661.	Y
575.	N	604.	N	633.	Y	662.	Y
576.	Y	605.	Y	634.	Y	663.	N
577.	Y	606.	Y	635.	Y	664.	N
578.	Y	607.	Y	636.	Y	665.	Y
579.	Y	608.	Answer	637.	Y	666.	Y
580.	Y	609.	Y	638.	Answer	667.	Y
581.	Y	610.	N	639.	Answer	668.	N
582.	Y	611.	Y	640.	N	669.	N
583.	N	612.	N	641.	Y	670.	Y
584.	Y	613.	Y	642.	Answer	671.	Y
585.	Y	614.	N	643.	Y	672.	N
586.	Y	615.	Y	644.	Y	673.	Y
587.	Y	616.	Y	645.	N	674.	N
588.	Y	617.	Y	646.	Y	675.	Y
589.	Y	618.	N	647.	Y	676.	Y

677.	Y	684.	Y	691.	Y	698.	Y
678.	Y	685.	Y	692.	Y	699.	N
679.	Y	686.	N	693.	N	700.	Y
680.	Y	687.	Y	694.	N	701.	Y
681.	Y	688.	N	695.	Y		
682.	Y	689.	Y	696.	N		
683.	N	690.	Y	697.	Y		

Bibliography

Matt Welsh, Matthias Kalle Dalheimer, Terry Dawson, and Lar Kaufman, Running Linux, Fourth Edition, O'Reilly Publishers, December 2002, ISBN: 0-596-00272-6.

Carla Schroder, Linux Cookbook, First Edition, O'Reilly Cookbooks Series, November 2004, ISBN: 0-596-00640-3.

Venkateshwarlu N.B, Advanced UNIX Programming, BS Publishers, Hyderabad, 2005.

Venkateshwarlu N.B, UNIX and Windows NT, BS Publishers, Hyderabad, 2005.

Venkateshwarlu N.B, Introduction to Linux:Installation and Programming, BS Publishers, Hyderabad, 2006.

Gary Nutt, *Operating Systems: A Modern Perspective*, First Edition, Addison-Wesley, Reading, MA, 1997.

B.W. Kernigham and R. Pike, The UNIX Programming Environment, Prentice Hall India, New Delhi, 1994.

Richard L. Petersen, LINUX fifth edition, The Complete Reference, TMH .

Shelley Powers, Jerry Peek, Timo Reilly, Mike loukides, UNIX power tools. BP Publishers, New Delhi, Hyderabad, 2002.

Michael K. Johnson, Erik W. Troan, Linux Application Development, Addison-Wesley, Hardcover, 2nd edition, Published November 2004, 702 pages, ISBN 0321219147.

Robert Mecklenburg, Managing Projects with GNU Make, 3E; Addison-Wesley, 2003.

Robert Love, Linux Kernel Development, Addison Wesley, 2005.

Ronald F. Guilmette, Compiling and Linking Under the Hood, February 2002, Linux Magazine.

Richard Stevens, Advanced UNIX Programming, Addison Wesley, Singapore,2002.

Don Libes and Sandy Ressler, **Life With UNIX: A Guide for Everyone,** PHI, New Jersey, 1989).

On-line Material

1. Open Sources: Voices from the Open Source Revolution, First Edition, January 1999, ISBN: 1-56592-582-3. URL: http://www.oreilly.com/catalog/opensources/book/toc. Html.

2. Michael Stutz, The Linux Cookbook: Tips and Techniques for Everyday Use, First Edition, 2001. URL: http://dsl.org/cookbook/cookbook_toc.html

3. Lars Wirzenius, Joanna Oja, Stephen Stafford, and Alex Weeks, The Linux System Administrators' Guide, December 2003. URL: http://www.tldp.org/guides.html

4. Richard Stallman et al., Using GCC, URL: http://www.gnu.org/doc/using.html

5. Brian Gough, An Introduction to GCC, URL: http://www.network-theory.co.uk/docs/gccintro/

6. Gary V. Vaughan, Ben Elliston, Tom Tromey and Ian Lance Taylor, GNU Autoconf, Automake and Libtool, URL: http://sources.redhat.com/autobook/

7. Karl Fogel and Moshe Bar, Open Source Development with CVS, Third Edition, URL: http://cvsbook.red-bean.com/

8. Mendel Cooper, Advanced Bash Scripting Guide, June 2005. URL: http://www.tldp.org/guides.html

9. Steve Best, Mastering Linux debugging techniques, IBM devloperWorks Journal, Aug, 2002.

10. Filip Rooms, Some Advanced Debuuging techniques in C Under Linux, filip_rooms@hotmail.com.